Wendy Weaver

Salt
of the
Earth

HALLARD PRESS

Library of Congress Control Number: 2023909505

Publisher's Cataloging-in-Publication data

Names: Weaver, Wendy, author.
Title: Salt of the earth / written by Wendy Weaver.
Description: The Villages, FL: Hallard Press, LLC, 2023.
Identifiers: LCCN: 2023909505 | ISBN: 978-1-951188-83-2 (print) | 978-1-951188-84-9 (ebook)
Subjects: LCSH Caregivers--Biography. | Nurses--Biography. | Women--Biography. | BISAC BIOGRAPHY & AUTOBIOGRAPHY / Medical (incl. Patients)
| BIOGRAPHY & AUTOBIOGRAPHY / Personal Memoirs | BIOGRAPHY & AUTOBIOGRAPHY / Women
Classification: LCC RA645.3 .W43 2023 | DDC 648.8--dc23

ISBN: 978-1-951188-83-2 (print)
ISBN: 978-1-951188-84-9 (ebook)

Contents

Dedication

This book about courage, selflessness, kindness, and love is dedicated to all caregivers, whether they work for an organization, help a neighbor, or take care of an ill and fully dependent family member or spouse. What you give is priceless. Never underestimate your worth on this earth and your donation to mankind.

List of Characters

LIZZIE	Agency Executive Director
ANNA	Agency Nurse Supervisor
MK	Agency Nurse Supervisor
MJ	Manager of Respite, Housekeeping, and Friendly Visitor programs
JUDY	Agency Financial Manager
LIDDY	Agency Scheduler
LINDA	Hospital VN
PEGGY	County Social Worker
DANIEL	County Human Services Director
ANDY	County Social Worker
MOLLY	County Social Worker
MADDIE	Visiting Nurse Executive Director
MARTHA COLE	County Department of Social Services Director

Aides

SANDY	STELLA
PATTY	GINNY
ANGIE	JANE
MARIE	HILDA
SUSAN	JODY
JOAN	CHARLOTTE
ISABELLE	REBECCA
CONNIE	ANITA
DONNA	

Introduction

SALT OF THE EARTH

It is my intention and honor to introduce you to a group of earth-bound home care angels by offering their stories on their behalf. The stories you will read are based on facts – real people, real events, real emotions. I was so privileged to know these people and to be involved in so many lives. The names of the characters in this book have been changed to protect their privacy.

Along with their stories are some of my own about the special times we experienced together. These stories may shock you. The stories may make you laugh or cry. Some may educate you. They will definitely put a new spin on home care and the people who happily cared for others many years ago.

I had been Director of a Treatment Center for adjudicated delinquent teenaged boys. After my maternity leave, I returned to the organization to work part-time in a new position created for me. However, when I reported back I learned that the organization I worked for had merged with another and my "position" had been eliminated. I was given a full-time position at a school the new organization operated for emotionally disturbed young children. While I did my best while there, I knew that I needed to look for a new job.

One day my husband was discussing my job search during lunch. His boss told him that his wife was on the Board of Directors of a nonprofit home care agency, and they were looking for a new Executive Director. He wondered aloud if I might want to apply for the job. Of course, my husband brought this information home to me.

I mulled it over a bit because I was very anxious to leave where I was. Between my junior and senior years in high school I worked at the County Nursing Home for the summer. I worked the 7:00 a.m. – 3:00 p.m. shift as an Aide. I was assigned to an area by myself and was responsible for the needs of eight women. I woke them, helped them to eat or fed them breakfast, bathed, and dressed them, transferred them into their chair, and assisted them with lunch. There were always diapers to change and general tidying including changing their linens. I remember some of those adorable ladies still today. How much did I love the job? I got in trouble for singing to them and getting them to join me in "Daisy, Daisy" and other old songs. I was sternly informed that singing got them too stirred up. Imagine.

So, in my remembrance of that summer job, I applied for the administrative position. I had no idea that the challenge ahead of me would improve a range of my professional skills and almost every other facet of my life. (And still today...)

The day I interviewed I remember doubting myself. "I thought, can I really do this job?" as I drove along the highway headed for the town where the organization had its office. I really knew nothing about home care. My first professional job after I graduated with a BA in Social Welfare was as a Social Worker at a VA Hospital. It entailed working with addicts as they checked into the hospital for rehabilitation. After that remarkably interesting and educational start in my career, I accepted a position as the counselor at a runaway shelter where I counseled both the runaways and their families. Following a year in that position, I returned to college and earned my master's degree in counseling. My next position was as the Director of the Treatment Center. True, I did enjoy the work at the County Nursing Home that one summer – but that certainly didn't qualify me as having pertinent experience to operate the home care organization.

However, as I continued to drive to my interview, I also realized that I did know how to manage a business. My father had been a businessman all my life and I acquired some of that knowledge by listening at the dinner table and probably through osmosis. As the Director at the Treatment Center, I had worked well with my staff and realized that I had some talent in mentoring and teaching others.

Looking back on that life-changing day, I had thought the interview for the job went well. I wore my pink suit which I found out years later had been a hit with one of the gentlemen board members. Another gentleman that interviewed me was a fellow college alum. Learning that broke the ice a bit and led us into a friendly conversation about the Agency and the position. I always felt strongly that a good interview was an intelligent and somewhat emotional conversation among the players. I felt uplifted as I drove home and reported to my husband that evening that the interview had gone well, although I had some reservations that they would hire me.

Imagine my surprise when I received a call later that evening offering me the job. I was so happy to have the opportunity to move from the somewhat belittling position I was in to a new and challenging one. But no one could have ever known what lay in front of me. No one could have ever told me that I was embarking on the experience of a lifetime – one that few ever have. I had just accepted the perfect job. A job that I would enjoy for seventeen years – and one that would introduce me to literally hundreds of beautiful people that have collectively and individually made my life full of beauty, awe, love, kindness, and wonderful laughter.

The Agency was a private nonprofit stand-alone organization that provided home health aide service and other social services to ill, frail, and elderly persons in the county, including Meals on Wheels, senior centers, and congregate nutrition sites.

The largest of the programs was the Home Health Aide Service. It averaged one hundred to one hundred fifty certified home health aides on the payroll throughout the years I was there. Other employees operated the nutrition programs. Sometimes the number of aides seriously dwindled to the point that we had difficulty meeting the community needs. Of course, the pay was just a little higher than minimum wage and in a wealthy county such as we were, it was difficult to recruit the number we needed. If the economy was good, recruitment for those low paying jobs was even more difficult. The staff and I joked that we were praying for a recession.

We frequently had large training classes in the summer when we could recruit college students. They worked well for us covering vacations that the regular aides would take. Some also worked over Christmas break. However, they would return to their college lives and we would be left short-handed again. I fondly remember those summer student aides. Several of them had been young men who we thought might pose a problem with our sick and elderly women. Lo and behold, the ladies asked for that "nice young man" more often than you would think!

Between the Nurse Practice Act, the state regulations and the fiscal impact of insurances, home health aides were somewhat limited in what they could do for their clients as opposed to what they were capable of doing. They could bathe, toilet and diaper their incontinent patients. They could follow care plans prepared by professionals that detailed personal care and routine physical therapy range of motion regimens to keep joints and limbs healthy. Additionally, we depended on home health aides to take care of the laundry, keep the house clean, do the grocery shopping and run necessary errands in the absence of a helpful family member or friend.

Home health aides were not allowed to cut nails, take blood pressures, give enemas, or prepare and give meds. Sometimes there were severe problems regarding these limitations. Drawing insulin and preparing weeklong pill dispensers became a nursing task if family wasn't able to take care of it – or, unfortunately, if family was not *willing* to take care of it.

For years, we had a bedbound client who lived in her daughter's home who had more actual time with our home health aides than she did with her daughter. The aides provided generally 4 hours per day around meal hours. This woman was precious. She was also a little devil when she would call me to complain about her Meals on Wheels offering that day! Despite being relegated to her wheelchair for years and then her bed for at least fifteen more, she reached out to help others on her telephone each and every day. Sometimes I still feel her presence in my life as if she is briefly watching and remembering me from up above.

Most of the home health aides went out of their way to help their clients. These people were not just "in it" for the money. That was immediately obvious. They were doing this work because they wanted to. You might say it was their calling. They were proud of their work and devoted to doing it well. Homes that were not clean became clean – and believe me there was filth in abundance.

Over the years, we trained and employed aides of all ages, in all shapes and sizes. I remember the women who came to a certification training class without ever having a job. Many had just sent their youngest child to college and were excited to contribute in a meaningful way to the community and experience some personal growth as well. Some were tired of selling retail because their days were the same over and over and over again. We had some young mothers join us who wanted to free themselves from the welfare world and earn their own living. I was always sorry that the company was not in the financial position to provide some type of day care for their children to make it easier for them. I was thrilled when occasionally these ladies found a way to go to school and become nurses. One in particular comes to mind. She had experienced a rough start to her young life.

We gave seniority awards each year at our annual dinner. Given in five-year intervals, we often ended with twenty- or twenty-five-year recognitions. I was always overwhelmed when I stopped to consider this feat...low pay, challenging work, dirt, odors, and human suffering for a living. Why???

Throughout the years that my financial manager and I devised, implemented, and worried over the budget of that organization, first and foremost on our minds was the payback to the home health aides. We generally managed a small increment in the hourly wage each year and by the time I left, we had managed to give some small bonuses based upon the number of hours they worked per quarter and partial payment for their health insurance. Never enough. Never enough.

I recently thought again about that reality. What prompted the thinking was a recent newspaper article from the local paper that I received from one of the nurses. A hospice client had just been treated to an airplane ride – obviously, something she had hoped to do before her life came to an end. There was a picture that accompanied this heartwarming article that proclaimed victory of the spirit. The picture was of the happy flier and her home health aide, Angie who rode along, standing in front of the airplane. Her home health aide was there to lend support and cheer this lovely lady. You can bet your life on the fact that the aide was there at her leisure. What was most outstanding was the fact that that aide had just phoned to say hello to me about two weeks before this article was printed. We talked for about an hour….and she never said a word to me about this event. It had been wonderful for her to participate, and I know that it was certainly not a problem for her because that type of giving and getting in return was almost a routine part of her life.

I would need no more than the fingers on my two hands to count the number of days that I did not look forward to going to work. Those ten or so days that I dreaded heading off to work generally required me pitting my intelligence and wits up against the political demons that held the purse strings for some especially important funding. However, I always had great support despite my wins or losses of those skirmishes.

I cannot end this opening without paying tribute to the people I was so blessed to have - the office staff that was of the same timbre as the aides. Caring, intelligent, hard-working, and fun. The RN supervisors had both the privilege and heartache of being in the field more than in the office, but they colored our lives so distinctly. Those people that stayed in and did the scheduling had the most stressful job imaginable. Other office staff managed one or more of the other programs of the organization. And then there were those that supported the overall system...administrative managers. Just as unforgettable as the home health aides, these fabulous people had a different daily stress – finding the way to affordably get suitable and carefully competent, caring and kind aides into the service of the persons who needed them. The picture always started with training but went on to require scheduling, monitoring, billing, payroll, regulations, and marketing. We all worked together. They were a team of individuals who worked hard and honestly with good intentions to do the job they were hired to do. And, of course, they had to deal with me.

I am many years removed from that organization, now; removed from the glorious feeling of productivity, self-assurance that I made an impact, and the warmth and respect of those that touched my life. But even if I don't routinely interact with them, they are still very real to me. I hear from them at Christmas or the occasional phone call. They are also sighted at the grocery store by friends of mine who then relate their news and well-being to me. I continue to follow the ups and downs of their families and hear about weddings and new grandchildren. And I also hear about their deaths. There are several who remain an active, solid, supportive, and enjoyable part of my life.

"Why *Salt of the Earth* as a title for this book," you ask?

Salt has long been a symbol for good. It has been used in several ways as found when doing research into how and why it has been valued.

The discussion of salt is found in several books of the Bible, referring to it in two significant ways. The Old Testament books of Exodus, Ezekiel and II Kings refer to salt as a purifying agent. Three other books, Leviticus, Numbers and II Chronicles, present it as a symbol of God's covenant.

In ancient Rome, there is found a different connotation of "salt." The Roman salarium (today's salary) was paid to a soldier for his service so that he could purchase salt, a valuable and highly desired commodity. Therefore, if a man was worth his salt, he was efficient or capable in the job he performed. Another source tells us that salt was used to ward away evil spirits. Rubbing newborn ancients with salt was believed to keep the child from being possessed by demons.

Today, it is widely accepted that if someone is the salt of the earth, they have admirable qualities and can be particularly relied upon. It can also be suggested that the phrase refers to someone who is humble and lacking pretension.

For me, the phrase always meant a hard-working, humble person who treats others with respect and understanding. They are of great kindness, reliability, and honesty; someone who not only believes in, but also lives the principles of godliness. And finally, I am thinking of the song that young children often sing in church when their choir is asked to perform; "This little light of mine, I am going to let it shine."

These people that I was lucky enough to work with, talk with and laugh with were the epitome of the Good Samaritan. The only way to succinctly define the fiber of these folks is by the title of this work. They were and remain to this day whoever they are and wherever they take care of others, the Salt of the Earth.

How do you ever repay these people? The answer became crystal clear to me one day as I looked at a photograph of a few aides and staff taken at an annual meeting; let everyone else get to know these people. The following chapters are my attempt at doing just that!

Lizzie

Lizzie

MY REMARKABLE TEAM

I WAS SITTING at my desk working on a quarterly report we had to submit to the Office on Aging regarding the service given during that time period. We had five different federal contracts through the Office on Aging, and each required this timely report. I was deep in thought using Judy's figures and fitting them into the contract service points legally required of us.

I heard the quick, muffled click of the loudspeaker that normally informed me that I had a phone call. However, what I heard was not what I expected. "I have an announcement. Due to lack of interest, today is cancelled," suddenly came blaring over the intercom!

Instantly, knowing the voice and remembering the early onslaught of phone calls, I started laughing. Anna! I could hear loud clapping from my floor and the one beneath. "Ah, take a break," I thought. Someone else then made an equally ridiculous announcement. I walked out of my office, down the steps, and joined the others, face to face, in joviality. Then, back to work. You could always count on someone to help ease the burdens of the day, whether work related or personal issues for some individuals. We all had our problems, and to know that there was always someone to support you was a blessing.

It was harrying and complicated to keep track of schedules, required nursing visits, etc. We had a whiteboard on the wall behind the scheduler's desk that recorded recent deaths. The information on that board was always acknowledged with facial and verbal expressions of sorrow, yet occasionally that outward emotion was quickly followed by a sigh and the mention that now we could cover another client who was waiting assistance. We tried to fill our orders as quickly as possible. We knew that most (if not all at the time) clients were either alone or with a spouse that was frail, ill, physically, or mentally challenged themselves.

MK was a great Nurse Supervisor and the other nurse on our staff, Anna, was just as remarkable in her profession. MK had been a Home Care Nurse for years. She was older than me by about fifteen years. She never colored her hair and wore it about shoulder length; straight and pulled back by bobby pins. She was petite and of average weight for her height. MK was warm and non-judgmental, with an easy laugh. If she was offended by something, she simply turned away. She had a warm and caring bedside manner and great appreciation for the aides who worked long hours doing a job that few were willing to undertake. You could count on MK. She always had the answer to your question or the needed phone number or address on a paper note, written to herself, in her jacket or sweater pocket. You could bet your paycheck that the handful of crumpled papers contained the information you needed. MK never complained unless it was regarding client care or about a community professional who was not doing their job. No one could blame her for that!

The true pulse of the office activity was actually the scheduler positions. Like police or EMS dispatchers, one or two of them (according to the need) worked almost without a minutes' break all day, every weekday. Scheduling an aide from a field of one hundred or more scattered throughout a rural county, each with an ongoing schedule already, was a difficult job. Technology had not yet advanced as it would in future years, so the home or office tele-phones and a fax machine were the Agency's sole communication lines regarding referrals, schedules, and on-the-job needs.

The phones were always ringing, conversations constantly taking place either on the call or to another staff person, often with a hand being held over the phone to create a side-bar consultation. Once inside the office at 7:30 in the morning, the faxes were read and acted upon. New referrals sent after a hospital discharge the evening before were always there, which meant the order had to be filled that day to align with Medicare guidelines and, of course, be there for the person who was sick or bedbound at home. And morning substitutes! An aide's four-year-old son is sick, her car wouldn't start, she was not feeling well, the snow was too deep, and on and on. There were many days (sometimes, too many) when an aide would call out with an illness, a flat tire, etc.

The chronic call offs also became known and when they were scheduled, there was usually a little voice in the back of the sched-uler's head that said, "Don't do it! You can't trust them!" In that case, if there was no other aide with the ability to do the job, the little voice in her head was dismissed. Travel time between clients was a great barrier to A+ service sometimes and also had to be considered. On a normal Friday afternoon, the tension rose for the scheduler who was also looking forward to two days away from the hectic and sometimes frantic pace in the office. Who would call off at the last minute? Of course, one of the chronic call offs who didn't miss a beat dialed our number again. The problem grew worse if the service to be filled due to their absence was that evening or early the next morning. Saturday shifts were especially vulnerable to the flu or this time, a headache. So once again, those aides – and there were several – who rarely said they couldn't accept an assignment were phoned to fill in for the "headache" that time. Often times, we all lamented that we were taking advantage of these good and faithful employees. Maybe we did - but thank God they were with us.

We did all the Medicare aide service for the Visiting Nurses at the time, which was a department of the hospital in the county. Our stand-alone organization was prohibited by the State from becoming a Visiting Nurse organization ourselves. Under contract with the hospital, the two organizations worked closely together since the Medicare orders for aide service came frequently from the Visiting Nurses at time of patient discharge. They occurred throughout each day but a bit more frequently on Friday late afternoons because of the upcoming weekend hospital staffing standards. When discharged, the responsibility for that person's care was transferred to home care and while the VN would visit to assess the client's needs at home and write a care plan, it was our home health aides who spent the necessary time with them to perform the duties required of that plan. It was critical to provide the care at that time of the transition to home where providing care was so much different and more difficult. Much of the time there was just one elderly or ill caregiver in the home when the patient was discharged, which made the situation for assistance even more urgent. So, you can see why Friday scheduling was always stressful and dire. Fridays could be a nightmare. And not always because of the job and the task at hand, but my team's emotional outpouring for the clients. They cared so much that they did their utmost to make sure they were properly cared for all the time. Seven days a week as needed.

Despite the call offs, the vast majority of the aides were dependable, hard-working, and very caring people. Out of the majority that worked three or more clients a day, the odds that a handful or less would need substitutes at any given time were not crucially high. Sometimes the timing was bad for the scheduler, however. One aide phoned off three times within a few weeks because a tree had fallen on her house! Of course, we began doubting this aide – especially me. She had always been dependable and honest, which concerned us all the more. We shortly learned that it was true when she came to the office with pictures of all three occurrences. It was obvious they were different trees lying on different areas of the house! We "roasted" her good-naturedly at the Annual Meeting that year as having the best excuses for calling off.

Another aide reported to work on the morning that her home had burned during the night. The kitchen was lost, and smoke damaged the remainder of the house. Sandy made it to all of her clients that day. "What could I do for the house? My husband was there to manage the insurance. I will get clothes and things out when I get home. We're going to stay with my mother-in-law for a brief time," she said to MK on the phone. She was a valued employee and was happy to show off her new kitchen after the rebuild.

Judy was our Financial Manager. She had gotten a bit of formal education post high school but had taught herself the ins and outs of accounting and her work ethic was impeccable. I had to make her leave early sometimes or make her take a day off when we agreed that she had only a little to catch up to do the following workday. With payroll, grant reports, taxes and monthly, quarterly, and annual financials for the board and auditors, she had her hands full. She also put up with me asking her questions and for her assistance, which was not just a sometimes occurrence. She had the information and ability to calculate service numbers that I did not have. We did have a close relationship which helped. We could each easily apologize to each other when warranted or gently scold the one that had earned our frustration. And we were truthful to each other. Example: The bills of a private client were paid by a trust officer at the local bank. This woman was quite difficult to work with and gave Judy fits over invoices, work accomplished, and so on. Judy was not one to get ruffled or angry, but this lady often pushed her buttons. I could sometimes overhear the tone of a particular conversation coming from that area outside my office door. Generally, when I heard the phone hit the carriage and silence fill the space of the muffled conversation, I knew who she had been talking with. One day, the trust officer had called with a question and required proof that the aide had worked the hours that were billed. Judy copied the time sheets that recorded the visit and asked a new assistant of hers that had just started the week prior to send the copies to the officer with a note. Judy had scribbled the note with pen on tablet paper that was to be typed and sent. The scribble went something like this: Dear Pita enclosed are copies of the time sheets.... (For those who do not know, Pita stands for Pain in the ass.)

A few days later, I took a phone call from the trust officer. She was incredulous and terribly angry! I could hear her screaming at me before I got the phone to my ear. "I cannot believe you have someone like that bitch working for you! Does she think I am too stupid to know what Pita means?? I demand that you fire her immediately. What kind of place do you run there?"

I always thought I could act and that day, I proved it. In my best professional voice and demeanor, I responded, "Oh, Mrs. (whatever), I am absolutely sick about this. You are right. This never should have happened. Please accept my apologies. I will report this and see that she is reprimanded. Again, this will be taken care of. Thank you for informing me." (Of course, I was the one I would report to, but she didn't know that.)

At this point, Judy was standing at my open office door. Her eyes were wide open, in shock, listening. When I hung up, she said "What did I do now to that woman?"

I answered, "Dear Pita."

Judy's eyes got even wider. "What???"

Then it occurred to her. She turned and called Linda, her assistant. "Did you make a copy of the letter that I asked you to type up and send to the trust officer with the time sheets last week?"

Linda turned and went to her desk, returning to my office with a sheet of stationery in her hand. On it was typed "Dear Pita."

Judy was now in panic mode, but I just looked at her and started laughing. I couldn't stop. We both got the giggles. I hugged Judy. "Never again??"

"No way, was the response."

Our team was one of passion for the job, clients, and aides.

Occasionally we had HR problems, but few. We had one or two aides over fifteen years that stole from a client. One of them willingly admitted to the police that she had taken around three thousand dollars in cash. Of course, she was terminated from the Agency.

Shortly thereafter we held our Annual Meeting which included a nice dinner for the employees and their spouse or guest. The gal that was terminated showed up at the event and even said "Hello" to me. Can you imagine my shock and unbelief? However, I knew her well enough that to send her packing would be a big mistake with so many people around. She had her dinner that evening that she believed she had earned. Go figure.

"Lizzie, do you have time to talk to me?" MJ asked as she stuck her head inside my office doorframe. I rarely closed my door unless I was working to make a deadline for a contract, required report, or when I was on the phone with a Board member. I had an open-door policy, and the staff always respected my time. "Sure," I replied. MJ came in and sat down. MJ started with us as an aide and was one of the very best in providing care and in being a dependable, honest, and caring employee. She was also always pleasant, most of the time happy with great energy. Best of all, MJ spoke her mind. Sometimes it set you back a little but when that was the case, it was always for a good reason. Over the year or so that she started working for the Agency in the office and not in the field, she quickly learned the different jobs that were being tackled; she learned not only what but also the how and why of the operations. She scheduled, she helped with Meals on Wheels when needed, she was the assistant to a program manager and was always there in a pinch. As an example, she lived closer to the office than anyone else. (Judy drove over an hour each way!) When it snowed, MJ always made it to work ahead of "open hours" to start taking messages, active phone calls coming in with call offs, and began trying to get coverage for those who had notified us that they were unable to get to their clients. Her husband would plow our driveway and parking area as well. I could always count on that – which was a Godsend to me.

"Lizzie," MJ said that morning, "I need something else to do. Can you give me a job that is challenging and one that I can learn something from?" When she started talking, she leaned forward over the edge of my desk. She was serious. I smiled and appreciated her. As luck would have it for both of us, I had just gotten a state contract that required starting an entirely new social program that would provide volunteer respite care. MJ jumped in with both feet, developed the operating system, recruited volunteers that were needed and had it rolling in brief time. She also managed the lean budget (State contracts were not hefty at the time) and all of the service reports that were required. Her team enjoyed working for her, and she represented our organization well.

Anna, an accomplished RN, was relatively new in the home care field, but had broad experience working in a hospital environment. Her diagnostic skills were keenly accurate. She had three years of medical school in Poland, where she was raised, but when she came to the United States, her educational credits had not been formally accepted. Being married, with two children, she needed to work and was unfortunately unable to complete her goal of becoming a licensed physician. Anna was a beautiful blonde with an enviable figure. The men followed her everywhere even though she was married and most of them were aware of that. Her beauty, however, did not affect her demeanor or personality. I always thought that she really didn't know.

Anna was also naturally hilarious, especially when she talked about her family and her mother from Poland who broke the King's English with every other word she spoke. Her Mom had little understanding of our often-used expressive phrases or slang. Anna used to tell us so many stories, mimicking her mother's foreign accent and the murderous use of some words. On occasion, at noon following a particularly difficult morning, I would run out to pick up a couple of pizzas, order the phones muted, and insist we all gather for a lunch break. Sometimes we laughed until we cried with Anna breaking the work tensions wide open. She usually engaged in her comic performances as she walked around the table where we all sat, dining. Then others chimed in with their silliness. We relaxed, shared, and enjoyed each other for that often too short lunch hour. Then, back to the phones, schedules, files, administration paperwork and overall concerns that we were adequately serving those who desperately needed us.

There were other staff in the office that equally embraced our mission work by operating and maintaining the quality of the county's nutritional programs. There were about ten of us in the office overall keeping the engine running with up to one hundred and fifty personnel serving hundreds of clients each year.

I was so fortunate to have a remarkable team. We all got along as well as friends do and, boastfully, I would say that all of us held our clients and employees close in our hearts.

Focus, intent, and passion. That is what we were about when it came to work...the worth and meaning of the Agency's purpose. We also enjoyed having fun together.

Anna

THE CHALLENGING SEVENTY HOURS

THE STATE ALLOWED the Home Health Aide Agencies to train their own people for certification which was mandated to provide personal care. We conducted three or four trainings every year according to current staffing and anticipated need.

Seventy hours of training were required. Those hours included specific education regarding the elderly, how to work with families, and general professional practices which Lizzie taught. Alzheimer's and dementia, which required special training aside from the other conditions or diseases which were taught during the necessary training of physical care, were given additional instruction much of which included deep conversations among the group. Additional training regarding other aspects of client care was given by me or other "guest" specialized professionals from the area, including physical therapists, and occupational therapists.

After the classroom education was completed, the seventy hours were satisfied by on-the-job training at a local nursing facility. Lizzie appointed me to manage the training instead of MK because I enjoyed the task and MK preferred not to teach. She was older than I and wished to be in the field performing her normal work, instead. Lizzie and I worked together to recruit, interview, and accept the right candidates. Lizzie was resolute that no one would be certified that felt uncomfortable or queasy about the job. She told them stories of the worst they might encounter to give them insight into themselves and the real world of home care. She didn't have to think long and hard to find descriptions of actual unnerving situations.

The ad for the classes was placed in two newspapers – one of which was local and published one time per week. The other was a daily publication that many people in the area also subscribed to. I collaborated with the person that took care of our marketing to work up an ad that wasn't going to break our budget but that had the words and phrases we hoped would attract a sizable number so that we could end up with our target number of students. I took all of the phone calls, explaining the job and the training required. The majority of the callers wanted to schedule an interview and my calendar filled up quickly with the time necessary for them. MK covered all of the required field visits to clients at the time I was preparing for and providing training. Most of those visits were required in a timely manner by state or federal regulations. She worked long hours to keep up, but she always managed.

The interviews were always interesting. I had to be careful not to accept the candidate just because we needed a certain number of trainees. That would be like shooting myself – or the clients – in the foot. When I was on the fence regarding approving someone, I asked Lizzie to interview them as well and then we would huddle to compare our thoughts and come to a mutual conclusion. That often proved not just to be handy, but we were mostly accurate in our decisions. One or two that we doubted per class, we accepted, and they worked out. However, we did make our mistakes over the years.

Lizzie always started the training session by welcoming them and then addressing them as the Executive Director. "Good morning, everyone, and welcome to the Home Health Aide Training Class. I am Lizzie, the Executive Director. I will be your instructor for several topics during these two weeks, but today I am going to speak to you as the leader of the organization." From there, she would proceed to discuss the history of home care itself and the mission of the organization. She informed them of the responsibilities of their job. Lizzie also acknowledged the questions they probably would have at the outset and told them that those questions would be answered during training. Finally, she would inform them of the overall operations of the organization and pinpointed those that they would need to follow as an employee. Lizzie was professional, succinct, and thorough in her presentation. They kept their ears open and eyes on her.

I will never forget one opening day, though, when one of my "mistakes" got through to the training class. Lizzie had not interviewed her, which you will easily appreciate. That day, when Lizzie started speaking and had uttered the words, "I am Lizzie, the Executive Director," one of the students in the back row stood, picked up her chair, turned it around so the back of it faced Lizzie, and proceeded to sit down. Lizzie and I shared glances with wrinkled brows. Lizzie did not miss a beat, though, and finished her presentation with respect for the remainder of the class. She actually taught for almost thirty minutes, making notes on the blackboard, and encouraging questions that she would answer as she spoke. The student with her back to her never moved. When Lizzie finished, she wished everyone a great learning experience and left the room. That was when the gal in the back stood up, picked up her chair, turned it around to face the front of the room, and sat down. When we broke for lunch that day, Lizzie spoke to the young lady. Without chastising her or just plain asking what her problem was, Lizzie simply asked her to leave the class. She was out.

The other portions of the training that Lizzie taught educated the trainees on the mental, emotional, and relational aspects of aging, dealing with illness, and families in chaos. She was a relaxed, informal, caring teacher when she covered these topics. Lizzie rarely stood still – she roamed the room, brought the listeners into the discussion, and encouraged role playing. She often found that a handful of the students had not worked closely with other people, much less having entered a stranger's home to provide personal care for him or her. There were those who were shy and or lacked the level of self-esteem which was needed to properly meet the client at the outset of their temporary relationship. Lizzie would demonstrate the best way to do so as she role-played the aide, and a student would act as the client. It seems a bit silly, perhaps, but some students needed a boost and a mentor. And Lizzie needed the Agency employees to represent all of us in a professional manner. Her overall teaching demeanor caused certain trainees to volunteer their personal stories in each of her different classes. Normally, several in each class had cared for a parent or other family member and occasionally they had cared for a spouse, now gone but not forgotten. Those stories were especially difficult for the student to tell and or the rest of us to hear, but also cathartic for the speaker. All of the personal stories were either practically or emotionally educational. It was at these times that the students realized their responsibilities and the significant importance of their job.

One thing you could always count on in Lizzie's classes - there was always time for laughter and getting to know each other. That, to us, was important since they would often serve the same client at various times.

My role as the Agency Nurse was to teach a bit of anatomy and the physical side of aging in detail. Regardless of the few that had experience in this caring realm, I had to start at the beginning with everyone.

I first profiled our client types. We had clients who did not require much hands-on personal care, but more supervision. Some needed assistance with the household chores, grocery shopping and even filling out applications for special funding or reduced rates. (Lizzie had funds that were means tested by federal or state contract and others that were not restricted in any other way.) We had clients who were very ill and bedbound who needed attention throughout the day and some sundowners at night. There were those who were receiving chemotherapy and we dealt with the lingering sickness it caused. We had clients who lived with their children who resented their presence and their aged condition and basically ignored them. We had clients who lived alone, were bedbound and lonely.

We had hospice patients including young children who were dying of cancer in their home and lying in their own bed. So many different circumstances, illnesses, needs, personalities, and environments.

Field nurses assessed the client in their home and generated a care plan for the aides to follow in caring appropriately for that particular person in that specific home environment. What might the care plan tell them to do? Bathe the client; they would have to learn the proper way to give a bed bath and grow to know when they could manage giving their client a tub bath which the person might badly want to do. I went over every detail to bathing from a basin or sink. Draping the client when in bed or chair. Using two different wash cloths for sanitary purposes. Which body parts to wash and in what order? How to properly clean certain areas of the body. Cautionary practices like checking the water temperature - especially if they were going to have a tub bath.

Additionally, I would instruct them re: other tasks that would be necessary - changing diapers, cleaning up accidents wherever they occurred, how to deal with an indwelling catheter or optional ways to deal with urine incontinency.

Our Meals on Wheels nutritionist taught the class about nutrition and the special dietary needs that may accompany certain conditions. The prepared care plan almost always listed cooking or feeding. For example: tend to nutritional needs; prepare a meal, follow prescribed diets, feed the client, and the importance of adequate hydration.

I demonstrated the Heimlich and had each student do the same. We always had a student or two admit that their cooking skills were somewhat inadequate, and we took them aside to assess just what "I can't cook" really meant.

The students also learned about equipment and supplies

including a wheelchair, a walker, and the Hoyer lift, which we had in the training room for them to use. I required each student to move me on the Hoyer. Our students also learned range of motion exercises and understanding how to safely help the client lift and pivot to a bedside commode. And so much more. Basically, the training never ended until the nursing home "practice" that exposed additional questions they had that required our answers. The answers needed to be thorough and clear to erase any self-doubts they harbored.

It was essential throughout the training that everyone concentrated on what they were learning. In the home as opposed to a nursing facility or a hospital, there was little to no help for the aide. Many of our clients lived alone. Some lived with spouses that shared their age range and physical difficulties. Some lived with their children who were often at work. The aide needed to be aware of and learn to manage matters that they may have to deal with by themselves. Of course, they could always call us – but they needed to be confidently aware of their job duties and how to approach them.

At the end of a Friday training session when we were all "done" for the day, I was going through my "training bag" and found two or three Texas catheters. We had discussed urine incontinency earlier in the day. We talked about indwelling catheters and the necessity of carefully cleaning around them and what would signal the need to have the catheter changed by a nurse. I cautioned them, as well, to inform the nurse of any other symptoms that might suggest a UTI which frequently occurred with the catheters. Other options regarding managing incontinency were also discussed. Being a little silly and, therefore, a bit unprofessional, I took the Texans out of my bag and went back into the classroom to end the day.

All of the students were sitting around the table chatting. Brenda asked, "My cat is due to deliver very soon. Does anyone here want a kitten?" I heard someone say very quietly, "not me." There was a very quiet echo to that from others.

Shirley was chatting with Robin as she was closing her note-book and looking at her watch, "I have to pick up my son at school after his ball practice today. I hope I can watch some of it." "Oh, good for you!, responded Laura. That's so important – to support your kids. How old is he? I wasn't working when my kids were young. I applaud you for doing both."

Catching my attention as I walked into the room, listening to these side-comment conversations, Kate purposely said to me, "My back really hurts. I hate these chairs." "Do you have a pillow you can bring next week," I suggested and moved on to take in the interesting social environment.

Another duo was commiserating about their growling stom-achs. "I'm starving" Marie piped. She continued her thoughts with her chair turned to Peg. "What are you making for dinner?" I am alone and have to clean my house tonight since I have been here all week. Maybe first I will stop at a fast food and eat before I dig into that."

Other discussions were difficult to discern but obviously, all were relaxed with each other, and relationships were being formed. Clearly, this group of caring people realized they had things in common. I always loved to see that.

"Hey, everyone. Before I let you go today, I want to show you another incontinence product." I announced. They all turned to look at me. I brought forth the catheters that I had in my hand.

"These are Texas style catheters to be used for men that perhaps have trouble with one that is indwelling. They are constructed of three pieces." With this I picked one up to demonstrate the struc-ture. "The latex sheath is worn over the head and shaft of the penis and feels more like a condom because it is thinner than the silicone external condom catheters. The latex sheath is connected to rigid white silicone tubing, where the urine is drained, and it is connected to a catheter insert. These three pieces make up the Texas style catheter: sheath, white silicone tubing, and catheter insert."

When I was finished explaining the catheter, I picked up the other one that I had. The latex sheath was huge! Maybe ten or more inches long and proportionately wide. I looked at it and pondered it for a bit and then, as my instructor's filter stepped aside, and I blurted out, "Well, this one was obviously designed by a man!" The room erupted. I began laughing so hard that I soon realized tears were running down my cheek. It had been a long week. I so appreciated this jovial reprieve that signaled the workday was over.

Just then, I recognized a familiar laugh among the others. Lizzie had come in to wish everyone a good weekend just in time to get trained on the Texas catheters!

Angie

THE SWEET CURMUDGEON

I MET Willie one day in the early spring when he was referred to our Agency. I somewhat knew about him because he received Meals on Wheels deliveries each day. The Agency also managed Meals on Wheels, senior centers, and congregate dining in the county. We knew many of the clients who were "shared" by the different services housed within our organization.

Once or twice, I happened to have a conversation with one of the Meals on Wheels volunteers coming out of his apartment after delivering food. Consequently, it was really no surprise when the office asked me to see him. MK or Anna would set up the care plan and supervise me because it was not a Medicare order, but a private client. I did not know what funding was used, but I was asked to see him three times a week for two hours each of those days. I was told he had all ADLs (activities of daily living for you who don't know what that means) so the work was basically custodial and home management of sorts. That was a generous order, however, so I knew there was a challenge to be found working with Willie. I liked thinking about it as I drove to see him for the first time. In my experience as a home health aide, a lot of the men that we saw that were not hospital discharges or Medicare clients, were those who were unable to grocery shop, do their laundry or effectively manage their affairs. I assume that would be the case with Willie, primarily.

It had been a long winter. Starting in October, with an inch or so of freezing rain, it had been colder than normal. The heavy snows and subsequent thaws and freezes, in between, made a week feel like two and two like a month. In February we were treated to a storm that dumped three feet of snow and brought everything to a stop for a day or two. Accidents were all over the main highway that traveled northeast of us. This highway took everyone south of us to New York City and the other highways north to New England. New York was OK for a day trip, but not much more for me. The city atmosphere is not really my cup of tea. The initial excitement of going to the city wears off quickly. The first traffic jam, honking horn and crazy cabdriver is enough, isn't it? And the price of parking if you can find a place! I have taken the bus sometimes, but to me, that feels like I am in the city before I get there. Too close. Too much. Not that I do not like people, I love them. But perhaps I hastily identify them by where they are and what they are doing ---- they love the hustle and bustle, sounds, dirty streets, chaos, and the overall experience of the extraordinary. Guess I am basically a plain, country girl who likes order, routine, cleanliness, and solid, meaningful relationships. I am basically content and happy being who I am and doing what I do. To me, it is not a monotonous life.

That morning, I was aware of how tired I was of wearing heavy coats and gloves. In this job they are essential along with boots and a shovel. Good boots! Oh, and a bag of ice melt! It was not unusual for me to find snow-filled steps at a client's home. I often encountered this situation, and it was not unusual to have to shovel my way to the home's front door. I was blessed with an old car that handled snow well. In the winter, by company policy, I could decline the rural jobs because of the dangerous roads and parking situations, but I always try to get to my clients. Some have good family or neighbors, but many have only the aides that come in.

Usually if the driveway is long and deep in snow, I try to find somewhere to park down the street and walk with my shovel up to the house. The company was aware of this – other aides did the same because a client living alone was common and they needed to know if they were safe if nothing more. There was always a worry about heating and food resources with the harsh weather.

I remember a job where my client lived alone. She could transfer herself and stand without help, when necessary, but basically, she was wheelchair bound because of her lack of physical strength and balance. She depended on a neighborhood teen to come when it snowed and clear the way for those that came to help her, which included me. Sometimes the teen did not show up before I was scheduled to arrive and so, the duty fell on me or she would not have had personal care or breakfast that day, among other things. I often made her lunch and left it in the frig for her to get. I was always happy to see her. Despite her inability, she always smiled and told me funny stories about her life. She also had a ragged old dog that sat dutifully next to her all the time. I guess in dog years, they were about the same age. He was a sweetheart and always welcomed me with his tail wagging and a kiss on the hand. I never forgot to let him out to do his business when I arrived and before I left. I am sure he had something to do with her cheerful disposition. Her pal, Skippy.

As I pulled into the parking lot on the day that I met Willie, the winter was fading away. Piles of plowed snow were all around, but the sight of them was no longer pretty. Those that once were white were now covered with the black soot of gravel, ice melt, and dirty water. The additional melting of the sun and the passing of cars throwing up the gravel that was used on the roads made the loss of the white beauty even greater. As I walked from my car, I remember being pleased to see the new growth that was coming up in the gardens at the front of the building where he lived. At the strip of lawn that grew along the side of the building, small forsythia bushes sported new green growth and perhaps a bud or two along their branches. Birds were singing and tell-tale robins were walking the grounds and putting their heads down to it in search of a big fat worm to start their day. Along the sidewalk leading to the main door, flowers were beginning to bloom. Crocus and dwarf iris. Bluebells we call them. I smelled no perfume from either, but the combination of the deep purple of the bluebells and the lavenders and pinks of the crocus were happy together and reminded me that it was truly the beginning of better weather and the hope that came with the springtime sunshine that day. It was 8:00 a.m. and even though the flowers had no scent, the smell of clean new life was in the air. My morning was starting off well! I smiled and said a quick "Thank you, God!" as I approached the entrance.

I opened the door and climbed the stairs. It was spring after all, and I had vowed to myself to lose weight and thought that walking the steps instead of riding up a floor or two in the elevator would be a promising start! My upcoming high school reunion was only a month or so away and I wanted to look terrific! My best friend in those days, Nancy Stone, always looked thinner and younger than I did and that always made me crazy! She was the most popular girl in the class because of her blond hair and slim figure – and big boobs, too! I was always a little heavier and did not have the chest that made boys follow me through the halls. Some things never change.

These were senior apartments, and the building was generally kept clean and well-maintained. Someone had just vacuumed the hallway and I noticed the faint odor of an air freshener, probably from a scented tablet or potpourri put into the vacuum bag. I noticed the spring decorations that the residents had placed on their doors. There were plastic flower wreaths of all sizes and colors. Several had big bows tied at the bottom to fancy them up. The old ladies loved to decorate their doors for different seasons and events – their personal touch was always involved, and it told passersby about the personality of the one who lived inside. You could always tell which tenants were talented, artsy ladies and which were those who perhaps lacked imagination or originality.

On tight budgets you had to be very frugal; but not so much as to do away with the colors and cheery thoughts these door decorations shared with everyone that passed by.

A new week begins, I thought, as I knocked on Willie's apartment door.

Willie's t-shirt was yellow and stained with a hole here and there. He had a rather large belly, yet his pants were too big for him, and he was using an old, worn-out belt to hold them up. He wore no shoes or socks on his feet, and I wondered if this was an all-day habit or if he hadn't finished dressing before I rang his doorbell. He was unshaven with long silvery white eyebrows that curled up like fine wire. Willie was coughing and sniffling as he answered the door. I heard a bird singing inside which was an unexpected but pleasant surprise. Looking at him squarely and confidently, I put my hand out to shake his. "Good morning. I am Angie Lang, and I am here from the Agency to help you. May I come in?"

The smell of grease and his morning bacon frying filled my nostrils and took me back a second. Nothing new, really. A bouquet of odors was something an aide gets used to, especially urine, stool, or rotted food, which this time was not the case. The singing canary didn't seem to mind the smell. "Guess he knew it was spring, too," I said to myself.

Willie noticed my interest in the canary and his song. "That's Luke," he told me with a smile on his face. He was proud of him. "He sings often. I can't get him to talk words to me, though." Willie sort of shuffled his bare feet a little and walked to his easy chair to sit down. I believe he was uncomfortable that morning. He didn't know me. Thankfully, that changed.

I wanted to get something done during this meeting. I made my own quick assessment of the situation and then read the nurses notes and care plan. I again thought about his bare feet that obviously needed attention. His nails were too long, yellow and had the telltale signs of fungus. I wondered when he last had someone clip them. The skin on his feet was very dry and needed lotion. I noticed the need for him to see a podiatrist was on the care plan. Luckily, there were several in the county that were willing to make house calls if necessary. When I suggested that he wear socks and shoes around the house, he just shrugged. "Maybe slippers?" I asked, as I thought that would be more comfortable and easier to slip into. No reply.

I knew that Anna or MK would be here sometime during this visit to go over the care plan with me and any questions Willie or I might have. Anna probably came yesterday after Willie was discharged from the hospital to talk with him, view the situation and prepare a plan of care (work plan) that she left the caregivers who were assigned to see him. I really didn't know why he was in the hospital, but I knew it wasn't anything to worry about. If it had been, the Visiting Nurses (VNs) would have had a Medicare order. This was somehow a private case. I really liked the nurses on the staff – actually, everyone on the staff. The Nurses, Anna and MK, were kind and smart. Very professional, yet gentle and sweet to the clients unless they had to emphatically address a type of medical suggestion or instruction with them for their own good. I thought this might have to be the case with Willie. "He's a true curmudgeon," I said to myself and inwardly chuckled. I had known guys like Willie before and always got them to open up to me. I hoped Willie and I could have that kind of a relationship eventually.

Willie was not disabled, but his mental acuity was waning a bit as was his ability or motivation to "do" for himself. That was clearly obvious as I surveyed the overall clutter in the apartment and pieces of food on the counters and dining table. Dirty dishes and cooking utensils were in the sink. The carpet had not been vacuumed for at least a week if not more and a thin covering of bird seed and a bit of Luke's poop was around his cage. I was, at the time, hesitant to inspect the bedroom and bathroom. That can wait, I thought, but it is inevitable that I will. It was not a stretch that Willie's ADLs were weakening and that he was not extremely interested in keeping himself nor his home neat and tidy. His mind still served him with the need for food, laundry, and those types of fundamental needs. But I worried that it failed him with necessary paperwork, money management, etc. I knew I had to work with him on those issues in the future, but again, that could wait. He obviously could use some help with rudimentary chores and self-care first. I found myself worried about his safety as I looked around the kitchen. For our clients, there was a chance, from slight to great, that they might forget they had something on the stove or spill scalding water or grease on themselves. Today, the stove was full of grease splashes from making the bacon I smelled earlier, along with drips and drabs of other spilled food.

"Well, what are you going to do for me?" Willie grumbled. "I need someone to clean this place up and wash my clothes. I throw them in a pile on the floor over there," he said pointing to a corner in his living room. "I can't pick them up and take them downstairs to where them washers are. They told me that you would go to the store for me, too. How can you do all that in the little bit of time that your outfit is giving me?" he asked with a tone of frustration and a hint of anger in his voice. I detected a sly smile on his whiskered, withered face as he bellowed these things at me.

I laughed to myself, "Well, it begins!" Somehow, I knew this relationship would be something I would remember for a long time. It was his way that I liked; tough but squishy.

Willie and I managed to get a few things straightened out on that first visit. It's always good to share expectations of each other to break the ice and establish a good base for the relationship and job duties.

In the next few days that I was scheduled with Willie, I helped him with all types of things and organized his life a little more so that he could manage his daily needs and chores a little better. I had a talk with him about the stove and we worked together to identify dishes he could fix himself to eat without use of the stove. I taught him how to use the microwave for certain things, which looked to never have been used. Still new. He seemed to like the frozen meals I picked up for him when I went to the grocery store. I bought him an electric water pot so that he could have hot water from equipment that shut-off automatically. He appeared to be grateful for that.

Although he had softened toward me a bit, Willie's personality was a bit like a cantankerous Archie Bunker, and I worked hard to ignore a handful of humanly demeaning words or phrases that he frequently uttered. Honestly, though, I would tell you that I sometimes had to hide snickers at things that I never would have otherwise. But sometimes you accept things from someone because of who they are, you know? I did normally take him to task for his nasty and sometimes bigoted remarks. There was an interesting cross-section of folks in the apartment house, and he noticed everything! Willie could and sometimes would gossip about any or all of his neighbors. He found fault with the old women and called them names that made me cringe. I later learned that during the same visit, he might say something half-way decent about the same person he was trashing earlier. "That cranky old lady down the hall is always complaining about everything and she lets her stupid dog run in the hallway. I know he's going to shit in front of my door one day! She needs to be thrown out of this place – her and that damn dog!" Minutes later, "Ya know, that lady down the hall with the dog, nice dog, makes the best bread and she sometimes brings me a piece or two."

It was very gratifying after a few visits with Willie to see a clean, uncluttered apartment when I opened the door and walked in. Even Willie was neat and tidy, shaved, in clean clothes with socks and shoes on his feet. With Anna's unique way of dealing with people, she talked a podiatrist into making an urgent visit to Willie and his toenails were now trimmed and well-taken care of. I was not scheduled to be there for that momentous event, but I bet it was colorful as Willie probably vocalized his pain and impatience with the doctor frequently as the work was being accomplished. In his defense, if he did loudly utter a word or two of offensive language, I am sure the foot work was not a comfortable thing. He never said a word to me about any of it, but one morning when I arrived, he stared expectantly at me, two or three times looking down very briefly, then up again at me. I had no idea what he was trying to communicate to me. "Dang you! Can't you see that I am wearing my good shoes today, Angie?" he scoffed at me. I had to laugh.

"Willie, you are the prince among men! You look great!" He grinned and let out a real snicker. By this time, I believe that Willie began to look forward to having the company of someone he knew that was dependable, consistent, and interested in him – someone who would help him preserve his dignity and permit him to maintain that all-important gruff exterior that did not belie his age and failings.

I began getting Willie more involved with his shopping list so that I did not have to use the little time we had when I was there in putting it together. He followed my suggestion and kept a running list of what he liked and disliked, needed and did not need. From there, it was much quicker to shop for a week of food that was satisfying and easy to prepare.

Every other visit, I ran downstairs (only skinny or lazy people take the elevator!) and put the laundry in first thing. With another trip downstairs, I would throw it in the dryer and then make the final stop to fold and return to the apartment during the last few minutes of the time I had there. Willie was still continent and had no trouble during the night, so linens could be done weekly. I did his towels more often because they did not dry well in his small bathroom and often, they lay on the floor instead of being hung on the towel rod. The one chore I still assisted with even though Willie was capable, was Luke's cage cleanup. Willie was consistent with food and water, but not so much the cage. When I remembered, I would write him a to-do note when it needed to be done and I was not scheduled. That only sometimes worked. But despite the cage being clean or dirty, Luke never stopped singing during the day. Willie covered his cage at night so they both could sleep.

One day I arrived to find Willie sitting at his kitchen table with papers strewn about him. His face was flushed, and his eyes looked as if he had been crying. He had not cleaned himself up that morning and I didn't see or smell the signs of a breakfast made and eaten. I was shocked and instantly worried about him. "What's wrong?" I asked. "Are you all right? Don't you feel well?"

He looked at me. "These damn papers! How can I answer these questions and fill this stuff out! I don't know how much money I get and what I do with it! I eat. I have electric. What else do they think I do? And it is none of their business! It's just not!" He was obviously frightened and zealously trying to guard his privacy – and his ego!

I felt so sorry for him at that moment, that I walked behind him and put my arms around his neck with a consoling hug. "It's OK, Willie. This is information that they use to see that you have enough money and that you deserve some services at no cost. Like me!" I chimed. He patted my hand that rested from behind on his shoulder. I felt his shoulders drop a bit as he relaxed. I walked around to the other side of the table and sat down, facing him. "I'm going to do one or two quick tasks around here for you and then we will get the forms filled out. No worries." And that's what we did that day.

You do wonder how these people survive this confusing maze of information and paperwork that is required for health and human service programs and needs-based assistance. Home purchasing, tax returns and stuff like that are usually tackled by younger people or those who can employ appropriate professional services. Seniors – especially those alone – find it more difficult for numerous reasons. Think about it. They did not grow up with the technology they are supposed to be using now. It is not second nature to them the way it seems to be for youngsters today. Excel spreadsheets and grids are not familiar to them, either. In this area where I work, the majority of older people were farmers or crafts- men. Equipment was not run by a computer that needed unique skills to install or repair. Manual work was primary.

I had a client once who lost her husband after a lengthy battle with cancer. As he became frailer and the meds, he was taking more powerful, I learned just by being around them that she had never managed money in any way. She had never written a check or even gone to the bank for cash or to make a deposit. She had no idea of the income they received or expenses they paid. It really shook me up for her. I took Lizzie aside one day when I went to the office for extra gloves and my paycheck and told her about the situation. A day or so later, MJ, the Agency's respite program director came out to talk with her. Subsequently, with the wife's approval, a social worker arranged for someone to teach her what she needed to know prior to her husband's death. That story is not unusual, really. This was a few years ago. If the client was then seventy years of age or older, the marriage and family was most likely operated on the gender roles of years gone by.

Speaking of Lizzie reminds me of another Willie story. While together, we cleaned, tidied, and straightened his life a good bit, but Willie retained much of his gruff, sometimes caustic, behavior. I had gotten to know him well enough to know when he was kidding someone, and they didn't realize it; some took a step back to start to argue with him if they took offense at what he said. Others became silent and walked away.

One day when I was scheduled to be with Willie, I was told that Lizzie might stop by with his meal. She was delivering Meals on Wheels that day because a volunteer called off at the last minute. I knew she did this sometimes to get to know her clients but, as she confided to me one day, Lizzie also enjoyed getting out of the office and seeing different faces.

I heard the knock on the door around 12:30 and I knew it was Lizzie. "Hi," I said as I opened the door, happy to see her there.

Lizzie smiled her well-recognized smile. "Lunchtime!" she said, looking at Willie who had walked to the door with me. Lizzie walked in and took the hot food container and bag with the cold food and milk to the table, where she placed them. Willie walked closer to her. He then characteristically uttered a comment about the lousy food that was always cold and sometimes looked green. He had more to say, this time a little louder.

"Who makes up these meals? Not enough meat and too many vegetables. I need more than them stupid little rolls and Jell-O for dessert! The soup is watery, too. And them people that drop it off are in too much of a hurry. It ain't right! With what you pay them they got time to talk to me!" His little tirade embarrassed me a little bit. After all, she was my boss. I turned and pointed my finger at him with a big frown purposely planted on my face.

Lizzie laughed. "Come on Willie – can I call you Willie?" No answer from him, but Luke took this time to sing his hello to her. Lizzie knew all about Willie after talking to other aides and staff nurses and realized that his bark was much worse than his bite. She continued, "You know those meals are quite good. I bet you don't throw much of it away! The menu is prepared with your nutrition in mind. Doesn't that make you happy to know that you are properly fed? And, Willie, the people that deliver them are all volunteers – they do not get paid. You know all this don't you?" Lizzie finished her retort by saying, "You're just trying to give me a hard time."

While she spoke, that smile came across her face. Willie laughed his guffaw and smiled as well. They hit it off and had fun which benefited both. Lizzie bent over the table, opened up the hot meal and sat the cold dishes around it and beckoned Willie to sit, with a bow and a wave of her hand toward the chair. She giggled. He began eating. Lizzie talked with me for a brief time, said her good-byes to Willie and left to continue meal deliveries while they were still hot and she, on time. She told me later that she told the nurses that I was doing a terrific job and that it was nice to see Willie's house neat and clean and him, clothed in a clean shirt and pants – with shoes.

I always enjoyed the little good-natured tiffs that me and not-always-grumpy Willie got into. He really was a great guy when he allowed himself to trust someone. Thankfully, I was one that he did learn to trust. For other aides, however, that came when I was unavailable, Willie had a sharp and opinionated tongue. He always complained to me about them and accused them of cheating on their time, not working when they were there, etc. I knew this was not true because it was obvious when I returned that everything had been taken care of. I tried to remember to say something to them at in-services or the grocery store if I saw them there.

As the months rolled by, I was still placed with him two hours, three days per week. I learned increasingly about Willie and his life as we comfortably talked to each other while I worked in his home.

Willie had been married and had two children, a boy, and a girl. He didn't see them much, but they sometimes called to check in with him. Apparently, they lived close by because I felt annoyance in his voice when he said he didn't see them often. At least they call, I thought. Many of my clients never heard from their children, even by phone or occasional letter. I could never understand that. So sad. And the endless hurt and anger felt by being ignored and forgotten can almost never be healed.

One day, because he never offered to tell me and I was curious, I asked Willie for more information about his wife. Who was she? Where was she? I didn't pry, but only asked the basics. He danced around the question a bit, then solemnly said, "She lives up there," pointing straight up to the ceiling above him. "She lives in the ceiling?" I said aloud, but really meant it to be just a thought. "No, dummy! She lives in the apartment above me on the third floor!" he bellowed. He was annoyed with me and obviously annoyed with the thought that she lived upstairs. He turned his back on me, walked to his chair, sat down, and turned up the volume of the TV. I was speechless, really. I didn't know whether to apologize, console him or ask more! Of course, I wanted the details. "They live in the same apartment house," I thought to myself and caught myself rolling my eyes. Silence overtook us. Even Luke didn't know what to sing. That beautiful blue bird just sat and watched.

I continued fixing him dinner – a stew that he could eat for more than one dinner, or we could stick leftovers in the in the freezer. I was making it in a Crockpot so he could just unplug it at a certain time and store for the time in the frig until he wanted to freeze what remained, if any. Out of nowhere, Willie spoke again, telling me that he and his wife were divorced. Sometimes when he saw her in the building, they would say hello. Sometimes, he told me, she completely ignored him as if they were strangers. After those brief words, we never spoke again of her. I felt sorry for him because he didn't seem to have any hate in his voice for her. Maybe sorrow for something that didn't have to be. I never really knew.

However, shortly thereafter, I was scheduled to visit Helen, his ex-wife. She really didn't need a great deal of assistance, but I did grocery shopping for her, took care of her laundry and some other housekeeping tasks because she said she couldn't physically do these things for herself. However, I did notice that she was able to attend "ladies" events which sometimes meant taking the elevator to the street level, getting on a bus, and taking transportation to a shopping center, theater show or movie. She knew the system. I wasn't with her long, but for enough time that I learned her side of the marriage story. First, she told me she didn't even know Willie, much less having been married to him. She said this with great confidence and declaration; standing with her hands on her ample hips or with her arms folded under her large bosom. It reminded me of a movie about an Italian family whose matronly head admonished her husband for staying out too late with the boys. "I will have none of this in my house. Go away. I don't know you anymore!"

For a long time, the Agency was never certain who was telling the truth between the two. But they did their due diligence. Willie was. They had been married. And they had two children who both lived in the neighboring town, not five miles away.

I will never forget those two, but especially Willie. That aged curmudgeon had such a soft, sweet side to him. He had been a manual laborer who went through life doing what he thought best. Of one thing I am sure, he made an impact on me.

I sometimes remember what Lizzie warned us against before we started this job: "As the Executive Director of this Agency, I need to talk to you about getting too involved with your clients...simply stated, don't do it! A compassionate human being can find it quite easy to do in this environment and it could become harmful or hurtful in some situations to them and/or to you." I occasionally crossed the invisible line as did many of the aides despite Lizzie's advice. (Truth be known, Lizzie did, too. Often from her desk and on the phone, but she was known by a number of clients and not just from her signature or a picture in the paper.)

A little over a year of working with Willie, he experienced a stroke; one he did not recover from. I went to his funeral. His children and grandchildren were there. Two other aides attended as well. Helen wasn't there. I don't know what happened to Luke.

As I drove home after the funeral, I cried. I missed the sweet curmudgeon and will always fondly remember him.

Susan

PEACE COMES FROM BIRDS

THE OFFICE PHONED me one evening to see if I could fit in a client two days a week. It was about a twenty-minute drive from me. Our scheduler, Liddy, said she would move my schedule around so that the visits could work with my current clients. The new client, Maude Hoff, lived with her adult, special needs son.

I really did not want to drive that far with all of the other traveling I had to do with three other clients that lived a distance from me. I did really like the small town where Maude lived, though. As I thought about it, I imagined I could do window shopping for a half an hour at the end of my time with Maude every once in a while, and maybe grab a cup of coffee at the restaurant on the river. The cozy small town is an idyllic spot with the river flowing around it and an old grist mill wheel turning along its bank. A quaint wooden bridge crosses the water just beyond the mill, leading the guests into the old town center. Small shops line both sides of the street for several blocks. Side streets boast river views accented by old Victorian homes and well-kept colorful gardens in the spring and summer. So, thinking about a stroll after work, I said that I would take the job. It was a Monday, as I recall, and I would start the following day. I knew it was not a hospital referral with

Medicare coverage, but service probably through a contract with the state or county. Sometimes a county social worker ordered those hours. Maybe my friend, Dana, may have ordered this job. We had known each other for years, attending the same high school and church. As I drove along, I remembered singing in the choir together and spending too much time fooling around when we were supposed to be focusing on the music. I found myself singing one of my favorite songs from way back then when I completed my drive. I quickly realized that my voice was not as it was when I was in the choir. Aging does change things. Thinking of my clients, I felt a little guilty that the only thing that bothered me at this age was the change in the pitch and strength of my voice.

MK was to meet me there the first day. I looked forward to seeing her. All of us were so fond of her. She has been around the home healthcare block many times in this county. She is very professional, especially with the clients, but also warm and friendly. With us, she feels like family. She is patient and easy-going, but very devoted to diligent care. Even if it is not a medical concern with someone the Agency is helping, she quickly shares her concerns and gets the information to Lizzie who is always at bat for human service issues.

Maude's apartment was on the second floor of an old clapboard house on the main street of town and accessible only by a steep set of old, narrow stairs. The store below her was a trendy clothing boutique with fashionable garb in the window front, luring the wealthier residents of the area inside to purchase something for an upcoming dinner on the town or a special event. Maude, living on the second floor and wheelchair bound, never left her home. Her special needs son, Pete, the paperwork explained, lived there with her. He had a job doing dishes and janitorial work at the restaurant on the river, which made it convenient for him to come home to fix lunch for the two of them and make sure Maude was OK. Obviously, the social worker determined that Maude needed more care than Pete was able to give her.

I was told that the door would be unlocked because it also gave access to customers for the shop beneath. Steps to the second-floor apartment were straight ahead when you entered. There was a sign on the wall just inside the door with the name of the shop and a large arrow pointed to the right, directing shoppers to their destination. I couldn't help myself as I stuck my head through the open door to take a quick look at the clothing on display. "Nice stuff", I thought! As I started up the stairs, I called "Hi, Maude. It's Susan, your aide coming up the steps." I didn't want to frighten her – there was no real door as an entrance into her home. The stairs creaked with my weight.

When I arrived in the apartment, it was obvious to me that Maude sat in her wheelchair all day. I noticed a musty odor of being closed up, but thankfully not the odor of urine that often greets aides as they walk into the house or clients' rooms. Maude's living room was not big but where she sat, she was facing a large window. A phone, a box of tissues and a glass of what appeared to be water were on a small table, close to the wheelchair. All she needed to be safe and comfortable was by her side. Maude did not turn around to look at me, so I walked aside her, and bent over a bit to look at her as I introduced myself again.

Maude had a wizened look; she was very thin, and her coloring was a light chalky gray. Her white hair was long with a bit of curl at the ends. It appeared as if someone had pinned it up earlier, but much had come loose and was lying on her shoulders and back. I noticed her large, bony hands which seemed out of place because she was so small in stature, petite as well as she was thin. The skin was stretched tight over her hands and had that shiny, see-through look that told of her age. Her yellow-brown nails were much too long to be comfortable. A nurse would have to trim them. Aides were not legally permitted to do that. "Maybe MK would have time today," I thought. Maude wore a thin cotton dress that buttoned up the front. It was made of a small, flowered print fabric and was, at one time, something she might have worn for church or a social affair. Now it looked almost threadbare. The adult bib that was tied around her neck was soiled and stained. From the looks of the tray across the arms of her wheelchair, she was experiencing difficulty feeding herself, with pieces and drips of her last meal still resting there. "Those nails could probably tell us exactly what she had eaten," I thought. "I cannot forget to ask MK to trim them!"

I imagined this sweet lady in years gone by and felt sad that those years had resulted in this state of affairs. I have often seen the sorrows of those that lived too long as they were trying to maintain a quality of life. Many of them are mentally able to recognize it and steel themselves, knowing there is not much time left to them. I wondered who she had been when she was young and if she had any other children. "Did they visit her?" I wondered to myself. Maude's means of entertainment was certainly the window in full frontal view of her chair. The view was pleasant; an old maple tree gave shade and resting and nesting places to numerous songbirds that regularly gave bright color to the picturesque view as they darted in and out of the scene. She smiled a bit at me when I spoke to her. She nodded her head as if she knew I was coming and that it was OK with her.

As I was thinking of a way to break the ice a bit, I heard the door open and someone walking up the steps. "Hi, Susan," MK said as she got to the top of the stairs and looked to see me. "I saw your car and knew you were here." I walked over and we shared a hug. "I haven't seen you in a while. I guess the last time was at an in-service," she said. I agreed and we walked over to see Maude.

"Hello, Maude! I am so glad to meet you. I am your nurse, Mary. I am here today to talk with you, and we will decide together what Susan will do when she is here to help you. Your Social Worker, Peggy, suggested that you could use someone around to assist you with your personal care and household tasks. We know Pete works and isn't home much of the time. Does that sound good to you?" Again, Maude slowly nodded her agreement.

MK proceeded to take her blood pressure and pulse and to ask her routine questions that might give us an idea of her specific needs and concerns. While the care plan was being formulated, I walked into the galley kitchen, just off of the living room to assess things there. First of all, I wanted to determine if it was safe, and the appliances were in working order. I tested them and found that they were and nothing I saw at the time created any concern. When I opened the refrigerator, I saw many Styrofoam containers within; some small dish-shaped with lids, some large cups with lids, and the typical boxes with lids that folded over and clasped down over a meal or platter of something. I opened several of them to see if they were fresh or moldy and bordering on housing a sickness. They all looked as if they were only a day or two old. It reminded me that I was hungry – they did look good enough to eat! I assumed Pete had brought them from work. Maybe they had been prepared food that was never served? If so, that was nice of the restaurant to allow Pete to do that and must have been quite helpful to the two of them.

MK joined me in taking a tour of the rest of the apartment, so we knew what had to be taken care of and what the situation seemed to be. There was one bedroom and one bathroom. The bed had been slept in and not made. Pieces of clothing were lying around on the floor and on the dresser. All men's things. The bathroom facilities were old but seemed to be in working order. It needed to be cleaned, but I had seen worse. Some cleanser and Lysol would take care of things. The towels were threadbare. MK wrote notes to herself and went back to Maude while I looked to see if there were needed linens, what clothes were available to her, etc. This was not nosey business, but things I needed to know to organize my time and to see that she was taken care of properly. Many of our clients had insufficient clothing and also needed other items to live cleanly, safely, and comfortably. There were several resources in the county that we used for clothing, linens, and other necessities. I could certainly find the time on a weekend to look for things she might need. While I was looking around, I took notice of the scenic interior. Old, flowered wallpaper was in the bedroom. It was faded yet sporting the remnants of mauves, greens, blues, and yellows. The bathroom walls were also papered in a light blue with prints of old homes surrounded with ancient oaks and gatherings of gowned women and suited men. It reminded me of *"Gone with the Wind."* The same followed through the door into the short hall that met the kitchen area which was white and needed a new coat of paint.

When I walked back into the living room, I saw that MK was sitting on the edge of the sofa talking to Maude, whose chair had been turned outward, into the room. MK looked up at me with a warm smile, then stood. "Maude says Pete sleeps on the couch, here – she pointed to where she had been sitting – and takes care of everything. She now says that she does not need us. I have suggested that you come to visit just two days a week and we will see if she might change her mind about that. I think a nice bath for her might be in order during each of those visits for a start. Maybe changing linens? Maude tells me she is able to get herself to the bathroom, but I see the cushion on her chair is stained. Perhaps we can be of other assistance there."

She bent down and took Maude's hand and looked at her with a calm, reassuring face. "Is that OK, Maude? Susan can start today."

Maude said, "OK." That was the first time I heard her speak audibly. Her voice was low and shaky. She spoke very softly as if she had been encouraged to – maybe even when she was a child. Her face was drawn; her response seemed tentative. She did not look at us as she spoke. MK and I exchanged glances. Both of us were troubled for her.

I walked with MK to the top of the stairs where we could talk privately. They were bare wood as was the flooring throughout the house. I had not noticed any throw rugs, thank goodness. "Maude must not move herself around much," I said to myself. "Without thinking, she could send the wheelchair straight down the stairs."

MK interrupted my thoughts. "I will talk more with Peggy about this situation," she said. "I imagine the concern here was also for Pete. Too little space for mother and son to occupy and I was aware that we were both making some assumptions about Pete's ability to care for her. I don't really see him bathing her properly or toileting her if she finds that she cannot do for herself at the time or has an occasional accident." I agreed with her on that issue and suggested that it must make Maude uncomfortable if Pete has to toilet or clean her.

MK went on. "While you were out of the room, she stood up for me and pivoted a bit. I'll try to get her a walker. I don't have a clue why she doesn't have one now. She might get up and move around more often with the assistance. I do feel as if something more can be done. I'll contact Lizzie about PT. We shall see. Meanwhile, I know you will make a welcomed difference." We smiled at each other and shared a goodbye hug.

I watched as MK walked down the steps and into the bright sunlight on the street. You could briefly hear the talking and laughing of shoppers and then the door closed.

As I was remembering our conversation, I made a mental note to ask MJ to find Maude a friendly visitor. Like MK, her name was Mary and to make it easy on all of us, her initials became her nick-name of sorts. We had an MK and an MJ on our staff.

MJ managed other, smaller programs in the Agency. Friendly Visitors, one of the services she managed, was just what you would think it was – the volunteers would visit their friend on a weekly basis. That might be a challenge for the volunteer, but how nice it would be for Maude after she got used to them being with her. "Shoot. I forgot to ask MK to clip Maude's fingernails." I said aloud to myself.

Maude and I spoke a little, while I stayed for the two-hour period of time. I sat with her, and we discussed the weather, the tree, and the birds in short, dry sentences. Sometimes she wouldn't comment but would just smile or shake her head as an answer to me. She did open up a little when she knew the birds and identified them as cardinals, jays, sparrows, and the like. We both enjoyed that.

I asked if she felt she had enough clothes, so she always had clean ones and she nodded her head, yes. Sometimes, however, they were not clean when she put them on, she told me in her short-handed way. I asked if Pete helped her dress, and she nodded her head. I did not ask about the bathing now. I cleaned her up in her wheelchair; washing her hands and face and making certain that the cushion was dry.

I knew there was food in the refrigerator for dinner. I made the bed and picked up the man's clothing. It was soiled from working and smelled of grease. I wondered how often these were laundered. I was hopeful that the restaurant spoke to him about his cleanliness and hygiene habits.

Before I left that day, I suggested that Maude use the bathroom first, in case I could be of help. I watched as she wheeled her chair in and stood up to move to the toilet. It was not much of a struggle, she groaned a bit with stiffness, but she was able to complete the task and return to her chair. The bathroom was large enough to rotate the chair around and move it out head-first. It made me feel much better to have witnessed that she could safely do that for herself.

I told her I would be back again on Thursday. I left all of the pertinent contact information for them to reach us if needed. When I said, "Goodbye and see you in a few days," Maude was in her original space, staring out of the window. No birds happened to be perched there at that time. Was she just thinking or waiting for them to show up? That was a Tuesday.

My week had been going very quickly and it was already Thursday. One more day and then the weekend. My husband, Gary, and I had planned to take Saturday for ourselves, no working in the house or yard. Maybe we would take a drive to a park for a picnic again, go shopping (although Gary does not really like to shop unless it's for cars) or have dinner and a movie. We would decide when we got up that morning. I thought lovingly of him as I was driving to Maude's. We had no children, which was a disappointment in our marriage. However, we really liked being with each other. Gary was a warm person and we often cuddled as we sat on the couch talking or watching TV. And we both loved our jobs. Things have always been good for us; sometimes better than others, but always at least OK. We did not fight and respected each other's time, talents, and interests. Of course, his is cars. Mine, gardening. I love to watch the flowers bloom, vegetables grow and ripen, and corn go into tassel. It is such a gift to have fresh flowers on the kitchen table. I think the best of all, however, is picking a ripe cherry tomato and eating it while it is still warmed from the sun. Yum!

I had trouble finding a parking space in town that day but managed to locate one two blocks from Maude's place. I hollered, "It's Susan" as I opened the door and started up the steps. Maude was again sitting in front of the window but had moved her chair around to see me as I got to the top of the stairs. She smiled and said hello to me. She almost seemed glad to see me which made me smile. Good.

I went over to her and held her hand. "How are you today?" I asked. She answered, "OK" with a nod of her head and another faint smile.

"Good. What shall we do today? I can help you with a nice bath, do laundry and make a grocery list for next week if there is time. How does that sound?" She nodded her assent, and I went off to the bathroom to get things together for her bath. There was hand soap in the tub. I found shampoo and conditioner in the linen cupboard and a dry, clean towel.

I then searched in the bedroom for clean underwear. No luck. "Maude, can you help me find clean clothes for you?" I called. Assuming she would help, I went out to escort her into the bedroom. "Here are my things," she said as she pointed to a small portable stand with drawers that was in the closet. "My underwear and socks are in there and my dress hangs up." There was one dress hanging there and a few pairs of underwear and socks. I picked up what I needed and placed them on the bed.

"Where are the dirty clothes? I will have to take them to the laundromat before the bath to get that started. We can bathe while they are washing." Maude pointed to a duffle bag beside the dresser. When I looked inside, I noticed his clothes were mingled with hers in the bag. I knew, then, that I would just do his, too.

Luckily, I knew there was a laundromat just across the street. A Godsend when you have such little time in which to do a handful of chores.

"Do you have quarters for me to use or do I have to get change somewhere?" I asked her. She pointed to a coffee can on a shelf in the closet. Thankfully, it was full of quarters and dimes for the washer and dryer. "Let's get you back in your spot for now, I will run over and start the wash and then come back. We'll have time to get the bath in."

I made sure there were no other clothes on a heap on the floor anywhere, found laundry detergent in the kitchen under the sink, grabbed the duffle bag and the coffee can and went to the laundromat. I was gone just a few minutes and got back to help Maude.

Maude's demeanor never changed, and she said nothing to me while I ran the water in the tub, helped her undress and carefully helped her in. I thought to myself, "I may not do this again. Sink baths from now on." I worried that she would fall, even with me helping her. The care plan indicated a tub bath, but there would be no questioning me if I found it too risky. Maude smiled and said, "Thank you," as she washed herself while I sat on the toilet seat talking to her.

I asked if she had other children. "No, we had just one boy, Pete" was her reply. "How long has your husband been gone?" I asked. "Left a long time ago," she said and then looked away and continued washing.

The rest of the bath was done in silence. I used fresh water from the spigot and a large cup to wash and rinse her hair. I carefully helped her out and dried her off. I noticed that she winced when I was drying her around her groin area. Maybe I unintentionally rubbed too hard with the towel.

After I helped Maude comb her hair and get the clean clothes on, we went into the living room and she sat, as always, by the window. I made sure she was warm enough, given her wet hair and then ran across the street to put the clothes in the dryer. When I returned, I found her sound asleep in her wheelchair by the window. I noticed a little drool trickling from the side of her mouth. "Ah. Relaxed," I thought.

So, I quietly worked, cleaning the bathroom a little. Pete must have been relieved that I had started working there, because it appeared that he was no longer cleaning up at all. I remembered on the first visit that the bathroom was in fairly good order. This day, the sink had dirty water lying in it, probably from his hands after his janitorial work. Also shaved off whiskers that stuck to the bottom and sides. The counter had the same dirty water on it, empty wrappers from two Band-Aids and opened containers of products used by one or the other of the two. The toilet had stains inside the bowl, too. There was an odor of urine, and I noticed the floor on the front of the john was slightly damp. "Guess he misses," ran through my head. After I washed up the sink, counter, and toilet using a rag and cleanser I found in the cupboard, I walked to the kitchen to look for a mop and bucket in the closet that held other housekeeping essentials and canned goods. As I was leaving the bathroom, I noticed that the small trash can there was full. I picked that up and took it with me to empty it into the large trash can in the kitchen. I made a mental note to ask Maude when the trash was picked up so that I could make sure that I routinely had it properly gathered.

As I emptied the trash into the large kitchen can, I saw wads of toilet paper with blood on them. "It was quite a lot of blood," I thought to myself. "That kind of blood would require more than two or three Band-Aids." I finished with the trash and returned the empty can to the bathroom. It occurred to me, then, that I would never have the time to do the floor and get the laundry from the dryer and fold or hang it.

"The floor will have to wait," I found myself saying aloud. It made me laugh. Maude moved a little bit in her sleep, hearing me giggle, as I got to the top of the steps and continued down and out the door. It was a beautiful day and I thought about the upcoming weekend with Gary. We still hadn't decided on what we would do, but I knew we would relax and have fun together regardless.

After I had folded the clothes from the dryer, I returned to the apartment. With a little thought and direction from Maude, I managed to put the clean clothing away quickly – both hers and Pete's – in the proper places. I looked around and patted myself on the back briefly, feeling that I had made a nice difference in Maude's day.

"Maude," I said loudly so she could hear me from across the room, "I have a few minutes left. Shall we make up the grocery list?"

"I think Pete knows what to get," she replied. Why don't you sit down for a while and take a rest?"

I sat in a chair close to hers and together we looked out the window. She pointed to movement on a nearby branch. "Cardinals are beautiful, aren't they? My favorite color is red." She paused a moment, looked at me and smiled, then turned her eyes to the window again. "Did you know that they mate for life, the cardinals? I always thought that was nice of them." Another look and smile. I was so pleased that she was opening up to me a little bit. And smiling. We watched the birds a little longer as we sat there.

"How long have you lived here with Pete? Did you have a house in the area when you were together with your husband?" I hoped I was not prying but I wanted to know more about this rather quiet, lovely lady who sat in a wheelchair, alone, all day. Waiting for her reply, I stood and walked over to her and noting that her hair was, indeed dry, I took my hands and fluffed it up a bit. For her age, she had a good deal of hair and it landed nicely with lovely shape. I thought she looked beautiful.

"My husband and I had a little house up the road. But when he left, Pete and I came here. I believe he still owns that house. Not sure. He was a nasty man and never treated Pete too good because he said Pete was dumb and did not account for much. Maybe why he left," she said and shrugged her shoulders.

Her attention went out to the tree again. "I'm sorry, Maude. That must have hurt." No answer came.

It was time for me to leave. I had one more client that day about a ten-minute drive from there. I said my goodbyes. As I drove, I could not help thinking about that lonely, sweet, yet guarded lady. I was sure that her husband had badly hurt her.

The weekend was terrific! The weather was perfect for us to spend the day outdoors. We had a picnic on Saturday at a state park near our home. We took chairs to sit by the lake after lunch. There were wooden tables, grills and pumps for fresh water as expected. We packed potato salad and hard-boiled eggs that I had made, then purchased Italian hoagies and chips on our way over. We had a few chocolate chip cookies at the house that I also put into the basket as a quick second thought before we closed the door.

As we settled in our chairs after we had eaten, our stomachs full, we watched some kids swim while their parents sat on the sidelines, taking it easy like us. We would go swimming later in the year, but for now the lake water was far from being warm enough! The kids didn't notice that their lips were blue but enjoyed the splashing and diving. Three of them were playing monkey in the middle with a tennis ball. One poor girl was always in the middle and was taking good-natured ribbing with smiles and giggles. Gary and I enjoyed their fun as much as they did. It was relaxing just taking in the sun, the sights, and the joy of children's play.

Monday, I was back to work with a full schedule. Four, two-hour clients beginning at eight a.m. I carried my lunch with me as usual. So often, that same sad sandwich came back home with me in the evening. That is why I always made a peanut butter and jelly so it wouldn't spoil. And I generally took an apple as well. At that time, my Monday, Wednesday and/or Friday clients were not particularly challenging. They all were mobile with the aid of a walker and needed minimal assistance with personal care. I monitored their showers or baths. One was experiencing mild dementia and performed activities upon suggestion. "Mae, can you comb your hair?" or "Help yourself to your lunch." During my visit, the daughter she lived with would run errands or meet with a friend for a while.

On Tuesday, I visited Maude again. This time, my schedule had been altered, and I was there from ten a.m. to noon. I hoped to see Pete if he came home for lunch before I left. I had never met him.

When I arrived, I was stunned to see how Maude looked in her window chair. Her hair was uncombed, the dress hanging crooked on her and stained and wet from her breakfast. There was no bib. She barely looked at me as I approached.

"Maude. Are you all right? Do you feel OK?" I was quite concerned, a little scared, and quite rattled. She nodded her head.

She was nervously rubbing her hands up and down her thighs as if she might have pain in her legs. "Are you sure you aren't in pain?" She shook her head, indicating she wasn't.

I sat down beside her and then she looked at me. I could see she had been crying. Her eyes were red and puffy. Her cheeks were also red, not the pale sallow color I was used to. She sniffled and tried to cover it up. I could not get her to tell me anything, so I finally asked if she wanted a nice warm bath (even though I swore I would never help her into that tub again). Something clearly was upsetting her, so I thought that might help and I could talk to her while she bathed. She nodded, "Yes."

"I hope Pete can fill me in," I thought as I readied the bathroom and started the bath water. I escorted Maude into the room, helped her undress and got her into the tub. As I turned my back to straighten her clothing and take a look at that dress, I saw her hold her crotch out of the corner of my eye. She then began rubbing the soap on her washcloth. "I'll be right back, Maude. I am going for your clean clothes," I said to her. When I returned to the bathroom, her face already showed she was feeling a bit better and so we chatted about things. I just rinsed her hair well so that it would look neater when dry.

"Are you ready to get out now? You look like you are getting cold." She agreed it was time. We moved slowly and carefully. Seeing the one leg get over the tub to the floor was not the worst of the endeavor, it was that second leg coming over as she leaned on me for stability and then while she got her balance on both of them working together. I carefully dried her off. On one occasion she winced. I was upset with myself, that for her my drying technique must have been rough. Two steps and a pivot later, she was in her wheelchair where I could dress her with just one more brief stand for her to pull up her underpants. I watched as she turned her chair around and wheeled out into the living room. Unfortunately, that time I did not notice the bathroom trash.

Maude had a large porcelain vase in the room which I had admired with each visit. It was on a table at the other side of the window. The porcelain was white, designed with amazing colors of flowers, leaves, swirls, and independent, fine brush strokes. Such a statement it made as each color stood out on its own, yet melded with the entirety of the work. I asked Maude about it, and she was almost animated in telling me. It had been her grandmother's. Her mother had inherited it and brought it with them when they came to America from Germany. Maude recalled a number of family members to me. She, too, loved the vase. It made her remember her childhood, which had apparently been a memorable one. "I have pictures," she said as she pointed to a box on the bottom of a bookshelf.

Checking my watch for the time, I decided a few more minutes would be okay to look at some pictures, so I picked up the box and brought it over for the two of us to look through.

There were lovely pictures in the box, mostly black and white. A few were sepia prints, which automatically told me they were probably taken one hundred or more years ago. One focused on two women seated together, clad in long dresses with corsets underneath, cinching their waists as was the fashion. One held a parasol decorated with a lacy fringe. The dresses were fancied with lace and pearls sewn in a pattern on the front of the dress just below the high collar. The dresses must have been dark or brightly colored because the hose that slightly showed beneath the dresses, as they sat on iron outdoor furniture, appeared to be white. "Perhaps waiting for the picnic to begin," I thought.

Maude smiled as she looked at the picture I held in my hand.

"That is my mother, Mary, and her sister – my aunt – Clara. Isn't it beautiful? "Yes, they were beautiful women! And those dresses. Can you imagine wearing all of those clothes on a hot, sunny day?" I asked.

"Are there more pictures of your mother in here? How about pictures of you?" She nodded a yes. "There are maybe two or three in there, I remember. You can look. Just pull them up. No order in the box." I looked over at Maude and I noticed color in her face as she reminisced while gazing at the ladies.

As I began to search through the box for a picture of Maude, we heard the door close and footsteps on the stairs. Maude's face immediately turned to stone, and she looked down at the floor.

"You must be Pete," I said to the man at the top of the steps as I got out of my chair to greet him. I held out my hand to shake his, but he ignored the gesture. He was taller than I expected, yet thin like Maude. He had not shaved recently, or at least that morning. His hair was a deep brown with specks of grey throughout, especially at what would be the sideburns. His stubble had some grey in it also. Pete held his head bending down a bit in a way that made him look unhappy or ashamed, although when he looked at me, he met me eye to eye. He did not smile. If it is possible to feel a countenance, his felt heavy to me.

"Yea," he answered. "I take it you're the Aide" he said as he walked past me on the way to the kitchen. I looked over at Maude and she had assumed her normal pose – still and quiet, looking out of the window.

Despite the fact that I was a little uncomfortable, I followed Pete into the kitchen to talk with him. He was pouring himself a glass of milk and pulling out containers for something to eat. "You feeding my mother?" he asked me.

"Certainly, I can. Do you have something you planned to give her today?" He looked at me and answered, "Not really."

"Well, when you are finished here, I will get her lunch together. Do you have an hour break?"

"No. Half hour." was his curt reply to me.

I left the kitchen and went back to sit with Maude and maybe find a picture or two. We had been having such an enjoyable time looking at the photos and choosing other photos at random in anticipation of finding one of her as a child. Maude sat quietly and watched as I continued sorting through the box. I found a picture of one of the ladies in the other photo sitting holding a small child on her lap. "Is this you?" I asked Maude. She nodded her head and made no comment. As I sat with her, I found myself watching the birds, too. A peaceful and enjoyable way to pass time. I wondered if the tears I thought she had shed this morning had something to do with Pete. It briefly concerned me then, but more so at this time. Her inhibited reaction to his homecoming was certainly noticeable.

I heard dishes and silverware hitting the bottom of the sink just before Pete walked from the kitchen into the living room. "Going back to work," he said and then headed down the stairs and out the door. I was aware that he did not say one word to his mother the entire time he was there.

"Is something wrong between you and Pete?" I asked Maude after the door below had closed. "Did you have an argument this morning?"

After a lengthy silence, she looked at me and said, "No. It's fine." Knowing I should not pry and that she was probably telling me the truth, I asked no other questions. It must be hard having to take care of your mother when you are working, and his learning disability would make it all the more difficult. Maybe it was an innocent mother-son argument that brought tears to her eyes and made her feel sad. "It would be settled this evening after work," I thought hopefully.

The remainder of my time that day, I fixed Maude a sandwich and cut up an apple for her. While she was eating, I tidied up a bit, checked on the food supply and looked to see if there were enough clean clothes and linens to last until my next visit on Thursday. When I discussed making a grocery list, she told me that Pete shopped on Friday evening. We could do that on Thursday, I thought. I did take the time to ask her what she liked to eat that we should be sure to include on the list. "Sour pickles. And ham and potatoes," she said very thoughtfully. "I haven't had them in a long time. I like the turkey he gets for sandwiches and the apples. I like things chocolate, too. Cookies." I made mental notes. I was sure I would remember her favorites for two days.

I gave Maude a little reassuring back rub before I left that day. She was a darling and I looked forward to learning more about her and brightening her day when I was there. Later, as I was driving to my next client, I thought about the situation a little more and decided I would call Lizzie or MK before Thursday to ask them for their thoughts. Then I started thinking about what to fix for dinner as I continued down the road, eating my PB&J. I had forgotten to pack my apple.

"Susan, how are you?" MK said as she answered my call the next day. "Good. Do you have a minute to talk about Maude?"

"Sure! Why?" she answered.

"I am concerned about her and her relationship with Pete. I believe they may have had a fight or may not be getting along." I then explained the situation that occurred Tuesday when I was there. "It was discomforting to me. She had been opening up and then she froze when he walked in. Why did Peggy make the referral?"

MK took a minute to open the file. "It says here that the client seems depressed that may be due to inadequate care, cleanliness, etc. The only thing it records about Pete is his special needs status and workplace. She never said anything to us about the relationship itself."

"Well, can you call her for us and ask some more questions so that we can maybe help in some way? If it is just depression, she needs to see a doctor. Oh, and by the way. Her fingernails need to be clipped and she also needs to have a podiatrist come. Maybe you can stop to do her fingernails when you are in the area and see if she tells you anything. Might not be a bad idea to stop when Pete might be there to give you more of a sense of things and not just what I am telling you."

"Sounds like a plan. I am often out that way. I'll talk with Peggy and Anna, too."

I felt much better after the call and knew that they would work together to take care of things.

It was Thursday and I had not received any information from MK or Anna. I called the office at seven, hoping to speak to one of them if they had gotten in early that morning. Lizzie answered the phone.

"Good morning, Lizzie! It's Susan. How are you? You're in early!" Lizzie laughed. "I try to do this most days, but there are times that I just can't. My son doesn't go to school as early as I would have to leave, so if the lady that watches him in the morning for an hour or so isn't available, I don't get to leave the house until later. I was just thinking about you," she continued. "I have talked to Peggy about Maude. She told me that she had noticed odd behavior from Maude when Pete was around, but it didn't seem to be anything worrisome." She paused.

"I don't know what I think, now," I said. "Can you or MK please come out and we can talk to her together?"

"Of course, we will help. I can get one or both of us out on Tuesday next week. Will that be OK?" Lizzie asked.

"It should be, I hope. If you can make it sooner, that would be great. If not, let's stay connected."

"Absolutely," Lizzie said. "We don't want her to be upset or depressed about something that can be managed." We hung up and I continued on to my first visit. I would see Maude in the afternoon, my last client of the day.

It was raining that afternoon. The normally lovely town looked forlorn. I found a parking space close by because the shoppers had apparently canceled their plans due to the dreary weather. I had to turn and shake the water from my umbrella through the open door as I was entering the building. My shoes were not terribly wet, I happily noted, so I felt OK walking up the stairs with them still on my feet. "Hi, Maude," I called. "It's Susan." A loud sniffle was her only reply.

As I was walking over to her chair by the window, she said, "Why don't you come back another time? I don't need you today. Go home." I was stunned and confused.

"Why, Maude? I know there is laundry to be done and bed linens to change. If you don't feel like a bath today, you can just wash from the sink. I can help." Another sniffle. She reached for a tissue and blew her nose. She was crying.

I was by her side now and I pulled a chair over and sat so that we could talk face to face. "What's wrong, Maude? Please let me help you," I said. Again, she had been crying for a while. Red, puffy eyes. Her upper lip was also puffy. I put my hand on hers and sat quietly waiting for a response. Her hand was cold, and her complexion was the grey that I had seen the first time I visited. I felt sick to my stomach with care and worry for her. "She hurts," I thought, "but not physically." We were quiet and still for a brief time, both of us staring out the window. I finally got up and told her that I was going to take care of the laundry. I got all of the dirty clothing that was strewn about, the linens from the bed and bathroom and put it all into the duffel bag (which was so full I wasn't sure I could carry it), grabbed the coffee can and the detergent and quietly left the apartment to go to the laundromat. With the washers running, I hurried back to the apartment.

Maude was still watching the birds. "I am back," I announced. "Let's get you cleaned up." I walked over and grabbed the handles on the back of the wheelchair and started to move her toward the bathroom. "No, please don't," she cried. She bent her head down and buried her face in her hands so that I would not see the tears streaming down her face. Her hands were shaking. She might have well been one hundred years old at that moment. I noticed a reddish color on the chair cushion. At once, I thought of the bloody tissue in the bathroom trashcan on the day I started. I left Maude and went into the bathroom. Again, I found wadded up bloody tissue in the can.

I walked back out to Maude and sat down straight in front of her, took her hands from her face and held them tight on my legs so that she would look at me. "Maude. What is happening? Is that blood in the bathroom yours? Where is it coming from? Do you hurt anywhere?" I couldn't think of anything more at the time. I worried that it was rectal bleeding. If so, she needed to go to the hospital. "Is it from your rectum, Maude? Does this happen often?"

Again silence. I almost shouted at her, "Maude. Tell me so that I can help you! Please."

She removed her hand from mine and held her crotch. Then she looked at me. We were eye to eye.

"You are bleeding from your vagina? Your privates"? I asked. She shook her head yes. "Maude, we have to take you to the doctor or hospital. Are you in pain?" She tentatively nodded that she was.

"I don't need a doctor. I will be fine. Please don't call anyone. I am fine."

"Maude, I can't ignore this. I am supposed to be caring for you and I must report anything that is out of the ordinary or that appears to be wrong. This is out of the ordinary and this is medically wrong," I responded. "If you won't tell me what the problem is or seems to be to you, I will have the nurse come out as soon as possible."

I called MK and happily she was not far away. She said she would be right over. I sighed a huge sigh and went to sit with Maude again. I thought about the laundry, but I was not going to leave Maude alone now. It would wait.

When MK arrived and approached us sitting at the window, Maude broke down and began to cry again. It was breaking my heart to see her so unhappy and yet not able to talk to us about it.

MK was wonderful with her. She tried to sooth her with comforting words and told her that whatever the problem, we would work on it together. After a time, MK began to try to get to the bottom of things. "Maude, do your tears have anything to do with Pete?" Are you fighting? Has he hurt you?"

Maude began to rub her legs again and her tears reappeared. She looked at me and answered, "Yes."

Maude gestured toward her crotch. She shook and cried more.

Oh, my God! The blood. My mind was racing and heart pounding. MK looked at me with both sorrow and horror in her eyes.

"Maude," she said, "Are you telling us that Pete is hurting you down there?"

She nodded. "Why haven't you told anyone before?"

"I can't tell on him. He's all I have. Please don't say anything. No social workers, please. He's a good boy." Maude again covered her face with her hands. Her whole body shook with grief and fear.

I had witnessed the worst and the best of the human condition on this job. There are times when you can be an integral part of making a life better. And there are times when you cannot do much at all to improve a life. We could not allow Maude to live in that environment after we knew what was happening in that home.

Lizzie was notified that very day. She made her call to a board member who was the Director of the County Social Work Department. The next day, Pete was escorted out of Maude's home. They found a place for him to live from which he could keep his job. I never knew what the legal system did with the situation or with Pete other than taking him away from his mother. Maude's social worker found someone who would stay with her until they found a bed for her in a nursing facility. I prayed that she would have a window from which to watch the birds.

Lizzie
ALWAYS A PLEASURE

I LEFT the office around six-thirty to prepare for the in-service meeting that started at seven. I had to take the cookies and cupcakes over to the church and put out the paperwork that was already in the trunk of my car. Anna and MK would be meeting me there and aides would start arriving early. They always did so they could see everyone else and talk with them about their work and personal lives. I was aware that many of them had become good friends by way of church attendance, school children, or Agency clients. Of course, client information was confidential, but between those who cared for the same person, valuable information was meaningfully shared.

It had been a trying day at the office, and I was looking forward to the evening gathering. I loved seeing and talking with the aides. I almost said ladies, but we did have a gentleman working for us occasionally. I had been working on the county paperwork that was due quarterly and also preparing for the upcoming board meeting. Both required me to collaborate with my financial manager, Judy, who was terrific at her job. I was also adept at the financial end of the business and writing budgets. But, with Judy, I could get the week to week, month to month, and quarter to quarter data that was required for the reports to both the county, the state, and the Board. The county human services director always gave us a tough time when assessing the need for grant money. Although the day was not particularly difficult for me, the hours had been focused. I needed time to step back from numbers and to unwind a bit. Getting everyone to settle into a seat to open the meeting was more challenging than sharing company information, but fun to do. Regarding the programming, Anna and MK were up to the plate.

I guess to say that the meetings were always fun and uplifting to me would be an understatement. Unfortunately, I was one of those women whose husband was difficult to live with and I was always happy for time that I did not have to spend with him, even though I missed the same time with my son. I dreaded weekday evenings, Saturdays, and Sundays. My son, and my job, and its people were my saving grace.

I pulled into the church parking lot to find five or more cars, as expected. I got out of the car, carefully lifted the box of cupcakes from the back seat and started walking to the building door. Two aides, Susan and Charlotte, walked toward me offering to help. "There are two other boxes in the back seat, yet. Can you get them, please?" I asked as they passed by. It was nice seeing their smiles. "Sure thing! Hi, boss," they chimed.

The evening was clear and crisp for this time of year. The stars were bright and dancing in the sky. This far from town, not much artificial night light diminished the view above me. I loved this area. There is more farmland in the area than exclusively residential communities. The area offers beautiful countryside in all seasons everywhere you go. Not far from the church there was a miniature horse farm that I loved to drive past sometimes on my way to meet others for a quick lunch. The same farm raised goats as well and in spring, the new ones would be running and jumping together in the pasture while their mothers grazed quietly and watched.

"Need anything else from your car, Lizzie?" MJ asked walking from the church to meet me. "Yeah. In the trunk, time sheets and gloves. Here's the keys," I answered. We exchanged cupcakes so that I could get my keys from my purse and hand them over. Cupcakes exchanged again and I carefully opened the church door and walked in while MJ went to my car for the evening supplies.

I will always fondly remember hearing the pleasantness of voices and laughter inside the meeting room as I walked down the hall in the church to get to the main room. I could hear Anna's laugh and knew that the beverages had arrived with her, and the coffee was brewing. Several of the aides who would show up that night had come straight from their last client and would need coffee or tea, at least. Most ate the goodies, too. MK, Anna, and I discussed months before having raw vegetables and fruit at the in-service and had decided to try that. The aides appreciated the idea, but it seemed to change the spirit of the gathering a bit. We went back to goodies and coffee. "No real harm," we thought. I preferred it because the meeting gave me an excuse to eat a cupcake or something else fattening. Yum.

The room we rented from the church was large enough to accommodate the number of aides that came to the meetings. Generally, we had between forty and fifty aides attend a meeting, but sometimes there were more. There was also ample space for the speaker to set up and roam around as they spoke. The six-foot table with stacks of empty time sheets, other information, and box after box of gloves was always set up at the door in the hope that no one would forget the important tools to use in care activities and to record their work in the field. Running to the office for these things was a big waste of time if they could stock up while at the monthly meeting. It was a large rural county, and they might live thirty minutes or more away from the office. Coming to the mandated in-services and getting supplies was a one-trip event.

The church was a gracious property owner and only asked for a small donation. Everyone was respectful of the space and left no trace of their short occupancy so that no one had to clean up behind us before their activities. The Agency's building had space for the staff only. We did have an additional outbuilding on the property that had two large rooms which we used for board meetings and aide training classes. It was comfortable and provided a quiet space but would not suffice for a larger crowd and speaker.

One day when I arrived at work following an in-service, I was faced with a big problem. I was unable to go to the in-service the evening before and was looking forward to hearing about it. I very rarely missed those events for several reasons, mostly because I was with my larger family that I adored. Anna met me when I arrived at the office. I was surprised to see her that morning because she often went from home to her first client visit. "Good morning, Lizzie," she said.

"How did the in-service go?" I asked as I began walking to my office.

"Well...(hesitation)...we had a bit of an incident. The roof over the door of the church caught fire from a cigarette that was not put out properly. The fire department came quickly and extinguished it. Everything is OK, though."

"What?? How bad is it? How much is this going to cost us? They will obviously throw us out, now. Who did it???" What a terrific way to start a day. Without waiting for an answer, I ran out to my car, started the engine, and drove the mile to the church. As I pulled in, I expected to see devastation, but I could barely see anything at all. As it turned out, the fire apparently spread slowly, and the fire department was swift. And the church repaired the damage. There were no consequences for the Agency, and I never did learn who could not properly extinguish their cigarette in the outside sand filled container. By the time I returned, Anna had left to begin her day in the field.

To maintain their certification, the State mandated aides receive a minimum of ten hours of additional training each year. Included within those hours, there were five or so mandated course topics, which attracted more attendees than others. The Agency employed up to one hundred or more aides. The numbers fluctuated according to seasons or years of national fiscal trends. In the summer, college students were trained to assume the work for vacationers or for those who had school-aged children. There were also a number each year that quit because the job was not what they expected.

Anna, MK, and I tried our best to prepare them for multiple types of situations and people. It was difficult to talk the talk, but harder to walk it. Telling them that their client may have soiled themselves through the night and be covered with feces in the morning when they arrived did little to prepare them for the sight and smell and the complex emotions they would experience when caring for them in situations like that. We counseled them about the realities of dementia and Alzheimer's and the complications of angry or frightened family members. I taught human relations training such as understanding the elderly, working with families of our clients, and the complexities of aging. Anna and a physical therapist colleague from the hospital trained the class in providing personal care, safety, and general duties. I usually gave the last class regarding the importance of confidentiality and company personnel policies that I had written specifically for the aides. Altogether, it was a 70-hour course that included hands-on training at a nearby nursing home.

The speaker at the in-service this evening was the Director of the County's Health Department who would educate the group on the very prominent existence of Lyme Disease in the area. Next month, we had scheduled a mandatory topic.

I hugged Anna. "Missed you today. How many stops did you have?"

"I did four first visits and three Medicaid visits today," Anna responded. "I did the paperwork at home this evening instead of going back to the office. I made a quick dinner for everyone before I left. One new client is going to be rather difficult. The family fought together the whole time I was there."

"Over what?" I instinctively knew situations like that are difficult for the aides to work with and around.

"The client, Mrs. Cain, had a severe stroke. She cries and screams and her family that she lives with has no patience for it. Son and daughter-in-law. When I was with them, they yelled and told her to shut up more than once. The lady's daughter was there to talk with me privately. She takes up for her poor mother which increases the tension in the house. Didn't get a good first impression of son and daughter-in-law. The house is very cluttered."

"What about Mrs. Cain? Is she manageable personal care wise," I asked?

Anna answered that she was if she was calm. "She is a fall risk. I wonder if her son and daughter-in-law will see that she gets her meds and food. And of course, she has to endure their impatience and loud words," she said.

MK, having overheard bits of the conversation, stuck her head into the huddle with her arm around me and asked if they were talking about the Cain's. I answered, "Yes. Do you know them?"

MK had lived in the county her entire adult life. She had worked in home care many of those years and was in real estate for a period of time. She knew every town and every street in that town. She knew many (with a capital M) families and had been in their homes for home care or home sales, rich or poor. She connected with people and families all throughout this rural area.

"What do you know about them?" Anna inquired.

"Well, daughter and son don't get along. I guess there was some money in that old place at one time that they must have fought over. But now, it's not worth much although there are five or more good acres there – maybe ten or fifteen," MK answered.

"In this county that could be a fortune," Anna said with a concerned look on her face. "Guess we'll have to assign the right aide in there. Angie or Marie could take it, I guess. The order is two hours, three days a week. I'd like to see that the aide went a.m. or early afternoon so she could make sure Olive was getting her food." MK nodded in agreement. Both ladies were at the in-service meeting, so Anna could make the assignment then. She walked toward Marie. Marie was kind and patient, like a sweet grand-mother who cared for everyone.

Karen, an aide that had worked for the Agency for a number of years and was well-liked by everyone walked up to me to say "Hi" and left to talk to MK about Mrs. Richardson who had just been discharged after heart surgery. MK had been out that day to develop a plan of care for the aides and Karen had questions. She was unsure about the foods Mrs. Richardson wanted to eat and thought she'd check. She also wanted to let MK know the family dog was not very friendly and that any other aides who might be scheduled there would need to know it. The Agency should have them put the dog in another room while the aides were there.

It was a few minutes past seven o'clock, so I meandered through the crowd of "Hi's" and hugs to the front of the room. I noted that a good crowd had gathered while I was busy talking and welcoming everyone. I glanced at the sign-in sheet. Good. Fifty-one tonight. Susan and Angie were seated, talking together. They were two aides that not only shared clients, but also had a social relation-ship and enjoyed talking about their husbands and Angie's kids. Great ladies. They always made me smile. I also noticed Joan and gave her a little wave. Joan was unique. She was beautiful as always. A classy lady, open to everyone and humble. She and her husband were professionals who had more income than they needed in life. Joan took the course to serve her community and did a fabulous job for us. She said she never knew how much she would love it.

I smiled at Isabelle, and she waved to me. I happily noted that her nails were short and unpainted. I was especially fond of her because she was a young single mother who was trying to make something of herself. I would never forget the day she interviewed for class...

Isabelle interviewed with Anna early that morning. I was at my desk working on a new strategic plan to present to the board when Anna walked in and took a seat. "What's up"?

"I just interviewed a young lady for the class and I'm not sure we want her. Will you please talk with her to see what you think about accepting her? We need at least fifteen for this class, but I'm not sure about her. She's downstairs in my office."

"Sure, send her up," I was always happy to interview and help the nurses with class interviews if they were unavailable or had questions. A brief time later, there was a knock on my opened office door and Isabelle stood there waiting. I waved her in and stood up to greet her. I shook her hand and she smiled weakly.

I could tell she was nervous. I never saw myself as any big deal, but people had told me that I was intimidating. I never understood that. It bothered me. I didn't know how or why, so I never figured out a way to control it.

Isabelle was incredibly beautiful, but also shocking in her appearance. Her almost white, flawless complexion reminded me of a fragile porcelain. Her raven black hair was full and shiny, like I had always pictured Poe's bird. (Wished that mine was!) She wore it long with natural waves. It provided a stark comparison to her face. Isabelle's fingernails were long, perfectly manicured, and polished black. Her black skirt and top might have been old or purposely vintage, but either way, were neat and pressed. To complete the look, her lipstick was also black. I certainly understood why Anna hesitated with this gal. "At least she doesn't have a pierced lip", I thought. We talked. Our conversation was helpful to me. She seemed to relax and enjoy our interaction.

To her credit, Isabelle made eye contact with me while we discussed her interest in the job. She was young. Regardless, Isabelle did seem to have maturity that might not have been expected upon seeing her. "I am a single mother with a three-year-old daughter," said Isabelle. She smiled and showed me a picture of her child who had the same pale skin and dark black hair. "I have been taking care of her at home with county assistance, but I need to make a life for the two of us on my own. I have always wanted to be a caregiver and I'm smart. I thought this course and job would be a good start for me. Hourly and part-time, I could make money, start a career, and need less than a full-time daycare placement, too."

As we spoke, I really liked this young girl and hopefully she was sincere and responsible. After a longer discussion about job requirements and business operations which Isabelle apparently found reasonable, I thanked her for coming in and told her Anna would be in touch with her. The class started in a week.

The aides were settling into their seats for the in-service and quieting down seeing me up front, so I didn't have to call them to attention that night. I thought they might still be energized by their excitement at being with the group and talking.

I welcomed everyone and asked for congratulations to Sandy, whose daughter had given birth to her first grandchild the day before; a girl. Everyone clapped for Sandy, who was an aide and did scheduling in the office occasionally. Everyone knew her and knew that her daughter was expecting. I then took care of organizational housekeeping and general information and requests. That was it for me.

Anna got up and announced our speaker, the County Health Director, who would talk to us about Lyme Disease. He had great slides with pictures of the distinct types of ticks, the look of the bullseye rash and a map of the county which showed that it had the highest incidence of the disease in the entire State at that time; the State, to make things more alarming, had the highest rate of infections in the nation! He talked a good deal about the disease and stunned us with photos of the worst results known of the infection. Of course, he advised us to wear long pants, shoes, and white socks when in the woods. Better yet, he directed us to not go into the woods or places where there might be a ground covering of rotten, damp leaves or similar matter. The aides had questions to ask, several having a client or family member that had contracted Lyme.

After I thanked the health director, I wrapped up the meeting with important reminders. Anna and MK also called the names of those they would like a minute with before they left. Not twenty minutes later, everyone was gone, the leftover cupcakes and paperwork were in my car, tables and coffee maker cleaned and I was locking the door to leave. The cupcakes would be a treat for the rest of the staff the next day.

I drove the forty-minute trip home remembering the evening and the folks that I loved being with and wondered who would meet me at the door when I arrived at the house. My husband's behavior was unpredictable.

Marie

SITTING IN THE SHADE

I HAD BEEN CUTTING back a bit on my Aide jobs so that I could spend more time in my garden – and also because I was feeling the effects of old age. It was harder to get the old bones to get out of bed in the morning. I wanted my legs to start working just after I put my feet on the floor. The hands sometimes went astray as they decided to work – or not to work – before my mind had a chance to give them my command really annoyed me. And my eyes required more time than normal to focus clearly on my room and the way to the bathroom in the early morning light as I limped, stumbled or sloughed in my slippers across the floor. I knew I should accept this as a normal condition, but I really felt disdain for myself sometimes. I realized that it was just a part of growing older but still chastised myself when I complained about my "aches and pains." I always became a bit impatient, and quite bored with those that wore their physical problems like a badge on their chest and I did not want to be one of them.

I did feel differently about my clients, however, when they spoke of their stiffness, hurts and worries. These people needed help with all or some of their ADLs and they, like so many of us, would prefer to do everything themselves as they did for the majority of their life. I was blessed at the age of seventy-seven to be able to work in my garden and enjoy the fruits of my labors. And blessed to be able to help those who could not do for themselves.

My husband and I led a happy life. We had three children together, so I gladly assumed the role of housewife and mother while they were growing up while Bill worked as a carpenter and builder. Living on a small farm, we shared the chores aligned with the care of a good-sized vegetable garden, lovely apple trees that annually produced a delicious crop, and five or so chickens that provided our eggs. I never found the courage to kill any of them to cook and grace our dinner table, so we fondly named our ladies, and they came running when we called them knowing that there was food awaiting them. Every morning, they made me smile when I called, and they came running with their feathered wings fluffed up a bit and their scrawny legs working into a run. They created quite the scene. I can still picture them in my mind's eye as I reminisce about the "old days."

Eventually, our three kids grew up and left home to build their own lives and families. Each did a wonderful job finding their role in the working world and choosing a spouse who not only loved them but also respected and enjoyed being with them. The grand-children are great kids. I have seven. The closest one is hours away, but they are surprisingly good with the routine phone calls. We talk easily about their jobs, their romances or someone who has recently caught their eye. None of them have yet settled in with a home or mate. I do feel assured that they will enjoy a happy, secure future. They all have good heads on their shoulders and kind hearts.

And, today, as I think about my approaching retirement from the Agency, my dear Bill has gone to be with the Lord and I work in my garden, feed the current girls, and worry somewhat about my future income. The retirement decision is a tough one because my work provides me with some needed funds, keeps me happily engaged in life, and my days are not boring. They are each unique in several ways - mostly pleasant conversations or comforting results of my work, having a good laugh with my client or seeing them make even the slightest improvement from the week before. Sometimes, the experience of my time spent with the client is a sad, lingering memory. Occasionally, they don't wake up in the morning and I get a call from the office before I leave the house. Many times, I have met their families who warmly put smiles on my face and thanked me for being there for their mom or dad. Working as an Aide can be very gratifying.

Last evening at the in-service, Anna approached me and asked me to take a new client – a two hour/three days who had just been discharged from inpatient rehab following a stroke. Olive Cain lived with her son and daughter-in-law who apparently were not thrilled to be the caretakers. Olive retained a low level of ambulation ability, but no speech. Obviously, she needed supervision and assistance for her safety.

I knew nothing else about Olive when I left home that morning and headed for her house.

The house was situated on a large piece of land – information that had been transferred from MK and Anna at the in-service – which was a property goldmine in this area. The house itself was surrounded by a groomed lawn, three or more flower beds and several mighty maples and oaks. As I drove up, I began to evaluate the property value in my mind. Significant, even though it appeared as if the house itself needed restoration work. The house did look like a sturdy fifty-year-old structure, however. White clapboard with a large front porch (both needing painting), it sported two stories with an ample number of large windows framed by black shutters. The front door was a dark turkey red which provided colorful interest to an otherwise plain profile. The rocking chairs on the porch looked well-used and inviting. I thought to myself that it would be nice if I could take Olive out to enjoy the chairs and the beauty of her property. My neighbor and I get together on my front porch to rock and chat outdoors. If it is in the evening, we might treat ourselves to a glass or two of red wine as we relax from busy days and enjoy our time.

MK also told Anna at the in-service that Olive's son and daughter-in-law were very unhappy that they were having to take care of her in any way. They lived in her house and apparently felt entitled to live there the way they wished – which was obviously having little to do with her. I understood that in a way.

Post stroke behaviors can be exceedingly difficult to deal with. She lost her speech and tended to be a crier/screamer. Very tough. I remembered a client I had long before who, after her stroke, could only say three words, "toot" "anon" and "no," but she fashioned them with her facial expressions and hand gestures in such a way that you could have somewhat of a conversation with her. She knew and understood what you were saying. Her laugh was infectious. I used to tease her that she needed a boyfriend and asked her questions about what she wanted her man to be. She thought it was hysterical and her "toot anon no's" were rolling quickly out of her mouth with playful excitement. We had such fun together when I was getting her ready for her day. But I digress.

Olive's single daughter, I was also told, was truly kind and showed love to her mother. The siblings unfortunately had angry discussions about Olive. I hoped and prayed that I would be worthy of managing the situation if I happened to be there when such a harsh dialogue occurred and perhaps act successfully as a mediator.

I must admit that I was a bit nervous the day that I first knocked on the Cain's door. There was no clarity about the situation, and it was up in the air regarding what I was walking into. But I did know I would do my best for Olive. One of my greatest personal fears is having a debilitating stroke. I wanted to help her.

The door opened to a large entry area that was reminiscent of older homes when the architectural style was immediately warm and welcoming to guests. This one had the customary area with a settee and small chair, both overstuffed and upholstered in a mauve and pink flowered print. The small table between the two pieces completed the look. There was a tall bud vase on the table. In it was a single pink rose with drooping head and dried up leaves. I remembered seeing the pink rose bush outside.

The couple that greeted me at the door introduced themselves as Harry and Nancy, Olive's son, and daughter-in-law. They welcomed me to the house with smiles and a relaxed attitude. "Perhaps the scuttlebutt was inaccurate," I thought and hoped. I introduced myself by name and Agency name – saying I was here to assist with the care needs of Olive.

"My scheduled hours are to be two hours per visit, three visits per week. These are orders which are paid for by Medicare. There are requirements attached to that funding which I imagine the visiting nurse (VN) has reviewed with you," I explained as the three of us walked into the hallway leading to other parts of the house.

Harry spoke as we entered what I assumed was the family room. A large TV, couch and overstuffed side chairs sat there with coffee and side tables that provided increased comfort to enjoy the entertainment. Decorations were sparse although a painting hung over the couch that illustrated an old Southern mansion and the tree-lined lane that accessed it. Very pleasant space. Shortly after the three of us entered the room to have a conversation I heard a loud wail from somewhere else in the house. The pitiful sound continued, one cry after another.

"Mom is very difficult to take care of, as you can hear!" Harry said very emphatically without any sense of emotion in his voice. "She cries and screams often. There doesn't seem to be any rhyme or reason around it. We have tried to determine if it happens due to a certain trigger – like hunger or thirst, but we can't tell, really."

Nancy went on to explain. "She was a very outspoken and nasty person before the stroke, so I think she is just yelling for no reason." She shrugged with a disgusted look on her face, turned away from talking to me, and walked farther into the family room to take a seat.

"I'd like to meet Olive. Where can I find her room?" I asked. Nancy got up and walked me down the hallway toward the back of the house into Olive's room. It was a small room, but sufficient. That's all I noticed at the time. At the sight of me, the tiny little lady with a soiled apron hanging around her neck from her last meal or two, started screaming, a startled and fearful sound but not quite as loud as her earlier episode. I walked up to Olive, held her wrinkled and gnarled hand carefully, and told her my name. I made sure my smile was easily detected as I looked into her face.

"Olive, I am so glad to meet you. I will be here to keep you company and help you three times a week. We will get to know each other and enjoy our time together. My name is Marie." As I held her hand and reassured her that I was there to be helpful, her screaming stopped. I remember that she even squeezed my hand a bit. She obviously understood the gist of what I said. I was glad to know that – our relationship would be that much easier. However, I reflected on the arguing among family that I heard about. "That must be very hurtful to Olive," I thought.

I heard the knock at the door and MK was invited in by Harry who answered it.

"Hey," I said to MK when we met just inside Olive's bedroom door. "So glad to see you!"

"Happy to see you, too," she responded to me. "I see you have met Nancy and Harry and Olive," she said as she looked down at Olive with a big smile. Olive accepted MK's presence calmly. She did not respond to her as she had with me.

We all found a place to sit in that room while MK went over the care plan that had earlier been developed by the visiting nurse. The VN was legally in charge of this client and the aide's work there. Normally, our Agency nurse would not come on the first day with the aide working on a Medicare case. I was a bit surprised but knew it was done for a purpose I would later learn. Our nurses were much too busy to make an unnecessary visit. We spoke briefly about my duties since everything was basically the normal plan anyway – bathing, feeding, incontinence care, range of motion exercises, meal prep when necessary and care of her room and laundry. In this household where independent others lived, I would have no responsibilities except for Olive.

"Do you have any questions?" asked MK when we stopped with the quick rundown hoping to discuss other things.

"I thought the aide was also going to clean the house, shop for groceries and other household chores," Nancy said with a stern look on her face. I looked at Harry who did not bat an eye at her statement. He did shake his head up and down in agreement with her, I noticed.

MK explained the Medicare rules with them which, I knew, had been told to them by the VN. This type of service was to be provided to the individual and not to family chores if they were independent and capable. Of course, because MK was from a different organization, Nancy probably thought she could pull a fast one.

I knew the Agency held to the same rules for Medicare clients, but when the client's care was funded from other sources through the Agency the aide was allowed to also assist the spouse who was semi-dependent or frail.

Nancy started the conversation regarding how unfair the rules were when she and her husband were so terribly compromised by Olive's condition. "Did you hear her yelling a few minutes ago, Marie?" she directed questioned me. "How would you like to have that around you all the time when you have to be in this house?"

MK answered for me. "While Marie is here, you and Harry are encouraged to take a break away from the house. Go shopping, to the park up the street, visit a friend perhaps? In this situation, you do need to return before Marie's hours are up. Make sure you use that time for yourself, though" she explained. "Doesn't your sister, Ruth, also give you time for yourselves?" she continued.

"Yes, she does. But begrudgingly. She thinks she should have the house when Mom dies, but we are executors, and we are keeping it," said Harry as he was looking at Nancy. Nancy smiled. Meanwhile, Olive had been listening to the conversation. When Ruth's name was part of the discussion, Olive made a low grunt of sorts. I had the feeling that she was unhappy with what was said.

But really, how did I know? "You barely know her," I thought to myself. That was obviously true.

MK was ready to leave. "Please use the tablet in the kitchen beside the care plan. It is to be used for notes between you, and Ruth, the visiting nurse, and the aides. I don't foresee anyone else but Marie to be here, but if there is a substitute for any reason, they will use that, too. If you notice any change in Olive, any concerns that are not immediate or just a thank you, please record it on that tablet. The aides will use it that way, also."

As MK was leaving, she asked me to call her when I had a chance. I knew MK would take an evening or weekend call if necessary. She and Anna took turns being on call, but for a quick question or chat, they were both generally available. I had also called Lizzie in the evening or on a weekend day when needed. I don't recall much about the rest of my hours there that day. I probably changed Olive's soiled diaper, exercised her a little and talked to her so she became more comfortable with me. I had been making mental notes about my future visits, however. I wished I could take her outside on the porch. But the porch visits needed clearance from the visiting nurse. It was just a small transgression against Medicare rules (the patient was considered homebound except for a doctor's visit), but I had to ask. I thought I would see to that after I watched her use her walker to know if it would be a safe move for both of us.

Two days later, I knocked on the Cain's door once again. I hoped I would get to meet Ruth, Olive's daughter today. In fact, Ruth answered the door. She smiled. Ruth looked like a Ruth to me. Medium height, thin but not skinny, light brown hair caught up in a bun behind her head. No jewelry. No makeup that I could discern. But a natural beauty. I guessed she was in her early sixties. To my memory there was little to no resemblance to her brother. My mom would have suggested to me that she looked like the lovely girl next door. When I was a child, I named my first "grownup doll" Ruth after the one in the Bible and my first impression of this Ruth fit my image of the one in the Bible.

"Please come in. You must be Marie," she said, still smiling. "I am glad to meet you. Harry and Nancy told me they liked you." I was surprised to hear that.

"How are you"? I asked. "I am glad to meet you as well."

I followed her into the kitchen. The kitchen was clean and neat. Nothing seemed out of place. No dirty dishes in the sink and the floor tile held a shine. We took seats at the dining table and chatted a bit before I would go in to take care of Olive. She asked me about my family and offered condolences when I told her that my husband was deceased. She seemed interested in my description of my little house, garden, and the girls. She also shared personal information with me regarding her life. She had been an English teacher in a local high school. Once engaged, she was sorry to say, however, that she never married. I was sad for her but did not inquire as to what happened. Heartbreak does not go away...ever. It might weaken but is forever remembered with sadness and the empty loneliness that encased you at the time. I was reminded, again, how blessed I was to have many years with Bill.

I noticed that it was quiet in the house, and I surmised that Harry and Nancy were taking their respite time and Olive was sleeping.

"Hopefully, Harry and Nancy had something nice to do today. Is Olive taking a snooze?" I asked Ruth quietly.

"I think Harry and Nancy did have plans, but I am not sure what. They like to go to garage sales and auctions when they can. Mom is asleep, yes, but she may wake up when she hears us talking. She doesn't like to be left out of anything! Inside, she is still a social butterfly. Everyone loves her and she feels very alone and rejected now – especially when I am not here. We aren't just mother and daughter. We have always been pals. It breaks my heart that this has happened to her. It frustrates her so."

I thought about Nancy telling me she was an outspoken and nasty old lady. Enormous difference from the picture that Ruth just painted. At that very thought, I heard a wailing from down the hallway. "I will get to find out all about Olive starting now," I thought. "She's awake"! Ruth echoed the general sentiment and we both got up and started toward Olive's room.

Olive, indeed, was awake and obviously unhappy that she was alone. When Ruth and I walked in, her wailing ceased. She looked at us with vacuous eyes that seemed to become more alert within a short lapse of time. Later, I could detect a light in those eyes that were framed with happy wrinkles from a life of smiling.

"Hi, Olive! I hope you had a good nap. Do you remember me? It's Marie. I am your aide here to help you." She nodded some-what...did she? If not, I knew that she did remember. I was glad to begin caring for her today so I could study and get accustomed to her methods of communication. I felt strongly that she was mentally able to engage with me in some fashion. I hoped that I was right.

I asked Ruth about the care that might be needed because I was unaware of any morning activity that would have prepared her for her day. Ruth told me that Harry and Nancy rarely bathed her and that she had not been in the home long before I arrived. I asked Ruth how she was normally bathed, and she brought me a basin, soap, and towels. Olive's walker and chair were nearby, so I began the process. I worked slowly and told her what I was doing each step of the way so that she would not become anxious. Ruth left the room and went to the kitchen to prepare their evening meal. She said she would stay and eat with Harry and Nancy. Olive routinely did not join them in the kitchen but was helped to eat her dinner in her room.

I talked to Olive very distinctly, but gently, as I told her that she needed to get into her chair so that I could bathe her. I wondered why she wasn't out of bed for hours during the day. Or at least that is what I had perceived. I didn't notice anything in the VN notes regarding any skin breakdown. I thought I would ask Ruth later if it wasn't an anomaly that she was still in bed this late in the day. I coached her in moving her legs off of the side of the bed and sitting up while placing my hand on her back to assure her safety. Olive, God love her, managed to maneuver this with just a little trouble.

She didn't do well on the first attempt, but on the second, I helped her to start her leg motion and she did it! She remained calm, but I did allow her to sit a minute or two before asking her to stand up with the assistance of her walker. She was a bit shaky at first, but once up and holding onto the walker, she appeared to be steady. After a minute or so, I coached her into a pivot so that she could take a seat in her chair. I felt confident in her ability to mobilize to this degree and hoped that walking a bit would be a distinct possibility. As I turned to go to prepare the bath water, I reflected that she hadn't screamed or made a sound while she was having to stand and move about. "Wonderful news," I said to myself under my breath.

The bath went pretty well although it was a bit apparent that she wasn't crazy about it. When I asked if the water temperature was too hot or cold, she answered with a nod or shake of her head. When I finished drying and diapering her, I went to her closet to find clean clothes. Her wardrobe was fairly extensive with nice pieces that would have been worn by a professional. It was clear that she liked to wear black and white but there were also blouses and tops that were very colorful. I chose comfortable looking pants and shirt that appeared as if both had been worn often. Black pants, pink shirt. Looking at the clothes it occurred to me that I didn't know who she was before the stroke! I was ashamed of myself.

Once she was dressed, I cleaned up from the bath. Olive sat comfortably and quietly in her chair as she watched me moving around. I told her I was going to leave her for a minute to ask Ruth where I could find clean bed sheets, which I did, and hastily returned. There had been no sounds while I was gone. Ruth brought me clean linens and I stripped the dirty sheets off of the bed and replaced them with the ones Ruth gave me to use. "Alright," I said out loud as I knew that at least Olive and her bed were both satisfactorily clean. Good feeling!

I helped her with arm and leg exercises while she was still in her chair. Then, we chatted. I said what I could think of to tease her into a laugh. The sound was not really a laugh, but a laugh was on her face and in her eyes. By this time, I was certain that Nancy's description of Olive was very wrong, and Ruth's was accurate. I was chatting with a nice lady who was living in an inconvenient situation; first the stroke and then the overwhelming results that ran throughout her life circumstances.

Driving home, I made two or three mental notes of the visit with Olive and hoped that I would remember them long enough to write them down when I got to the house. Only one client that day and I was tired. I hated that. Friends of mine who do not work at all say they have to nap every day. When I start running low on energy, I make myself do another activity that takes my mind in another direction and reenergizes me.

On the days that I was not with Olive that week, I accepted two substitute jobs. Both were quite easy. One required a grocery store visit and laundry only. The other was a morning assignment that required breakfast prep, transferring to a commode and then to the chair. She needed no help with her eating.

On my next visit with Olive that week, she began screaming as soon as she saw me in the hallway, approaching the open door of her room. I walked to her and held her hand as I had before and talked softly with her. She quieted. That day, I took advantage of the fact that she was in bed and worked with her doing other range of motion exercises than I did the visit prior. Her legs were not as weak as I anticipated. I wondered if she had been an athlete of sorts. Overall, the exercises went very well. She did not protest or express any fear. I was pleased that she trusted me. Together, we got her up out of bed. She pivoted around to take a seat in her chair. She smiled as she sat down.

I needed to talk with the visiting nurse and/or Nancy and Harry soon. "This woman should be out of bed during the day unless she tires," I thought. Per the last visit, I bathed, diapered, and clothed her. I talked to her, and as usual she made sounds indicating her thoughts or feelings. Some were low, some high pitched, but no wailing or screaming. After I cleaned up from the bath and removed the dirty clothes, I asked Olive if she could try walking a few steps. I mimicked her walking behind the invisible walker that my two hands were holding onto with my elbows bent. She made her sound of laughter and nodded. I assured her that I would hold onto her from the back of her pants. Olive stood up. I held up my hand to encourage her to take a minute to adjust and steady herself. She understood. When I put my hand down, I walked to her side, put my hand on the waistband of her pants. Feeling that, she ventured a step. Then another. Then another. And yet, another!

When she stopped for a rest, I removed my hand from her and clapped. A happy look came across that face and her eyes glistened. What a moment! Once rested, I encouraged Olive to continue walking. She made it to the hallway, pivoted slowly around and returned to rest in her chair. I was shocked and thrilled and so was she! I told her we could practice every visit until she is able to get to that front door onto the porch! (I did get permission from the VN.) I was almost dizzy with hope that Olive could enjoy the fresh air and the beautiful property that was surrounding the house that belonged to her!

When I left that day, I said nothing about the walk to Harry and Nancy. I was fearful they would take advantage of her mobility which might lead to injury. Negative thoughts about those two raced through my mind. I did my best to shoo them away.

I looked forward to the weekend as I drove to Olive's on Friday. Nothing exciting was happening for me but the weather looked to be good, and I would enjoy working outside a bit. Actually, I thought about sleeping late on Saturday but scolded myself – the one that disapproved of afternoon naps! However, I thought, sleeping in a bit was not as bad as taking a nap once your day is in drive. I put the late a.m. hour into my mind that did then, and still does, have an automatic alarm for 5:00 a.m. or earlier. I hoped to temporarily replace it.

When I arrived at Olive's, Ruth greeted me at the door with a look of concern on her face. "Harry and Nancy were not here when I arrived. Olive was screaming continuously. She is standing with her walker away from the bed and her chair. She has no clothes on, just a soiled diaper. Help me!" It was then that I, too, heard her wailing and I realized that Ruth had arrived just ahead of me, and the situation was current!

Together, we hurried to her room. Olive was still wailing, crying and pale as a ghost. I wondered how long she had been left standing to hold herself up on the walker. I quickly removed the diaper, draped her chair with a clean towel, and Ruth and I moved her gently and slowly to her chair. She sat down with an enormous sigh (a sigh is a sigh) and continued crying.

Only Heaven knows what went on in that room that morning. The odor was horrific. The bed sheets were half off of the bed, partially on the floor. Olive's pillow was on the floor. Her night-clothes were nowhere that I could see. I wondered when she might have soiled herself – during the night or in the morning when something lousy occurred? And where are Harry and Nancy?

Ruth went to work in the kitchen to fix Olive something to eat and a cup of decaf coffee while I began to soothe Olive with a calming chat. We both smelled the coffee, and it made us both feel a little like normalcy had returned to the day. I washed her with warm soapy water, rinsed her, dried her, and dressed her nicely. I found a red blouse in the closet that she could wear with black pants. I also peeked into all of her dresser drawers and found pretty jewelry. I chose a silver necklace that suited the red blouse perfectly. Her hair was very lovely normally, so I brushed it nicely and she looked like she had a lunch date! Afterward, she was comfortably seated so that she could rest. I mumbled to myself about the two adults who were enjoying themselves somewhere after doing something like this to Olive. Where do people like this come from? I stripped the bed and put clean sheets on it. And yes, as I was working, I was cursing those two adults in my head. The anger was welling to the top.

Olive, I learned that day, had a social worker with the county. Lizzie contacted them right away after I phoned her to report what I found. She also notified the VN who would come to check things out and talk with Harry and Nancy. The two were still not home when my visit was over. Ruth stayed and I did not know until my next visit what had transpired with the VN and social worker after I left.

The weather over the weekend was wonderful! I slept in an hour or so past my normal time to rouse myself and start a new day. I worked in the garden a bit, readying it for planting. I spent time determining what vegetables I would include this year other than the usual tomatoes, cucumbers, peppers, and corn, and deciding on a layout within which I would plant annuals among the veggies. I always used sunflowers and cosmos of all colors. Butterflies would frequent the blooms and add to the beauty of the garden. Not only did I relish the fresh vegetables, but I also had the opportunity to pick a bouquet and bring it into the house to enjoy. However, no matter if I was in the garden, watching TV or at church that Sunday, I was thinking of Olive and wondered what transpired after the social worker became involved on Friday after that freakish event.

I was welcomed by Ruth on Monday when I arrived at the Cain house. The house was quiet. I assumed that Nancy and Harry were not there – and I was correct. They left early that morning after Ruth arrived. She was to stay for the entire day while they enjoyed time away from home and Olive's care. Ruth was perky and happy, as she always seemed to be.

"Olive has had her breakfast already and I was able to assist her into her chair," Ruth reported to me with a smile. "She is fine this morning – maybe even happy," she said.

"What happened Friday and the weekend?" I asked anxiously. "I worried about her all weekend and hoped that Nancy and Harry would be realizing the consequences for their actions. What really happened that day?"

Ruth answered without pause. "They told the social worker – Molly, I think – that Mom woke them early in the morning, screaming, and she would not stop no matter how they tried to quiet her. They thought that getting her out of bed and into the chair might help. Together they tried to pick her up to get her out of bed. She began a wailing cry and fought their efforts to lift her. Sitting up did not change anything so they undressed her. They intended to clean her and put on a fresh diaper. This was the story they offered up to Molly, saying at this point, that they simply could not stand the noises another minute and they left her sitting in the chair, unclothed. I suppose that Mom got herself up into the walker and then did not know what to do or where to go. She was probably exhausted from the angst and her body obviously expressed the emotion."

Apparently, Molly sympathized with Nancy and Harry and arranged for additional help over the weekend and during this week so they could get away from the situation. I was not happy about this for it felt like Nancy and Harry were being rewarded, but I was glad that Olive did not have to deal with them except during the hours she would be sleeping, hopefully. I wondered if this additional freedom would soften the two caregivers or make them even more disdainful of their mother.

Looking back on that week that Nancy and Harry lived their reprieve, Olive made strides with her ambulation under my careful assistance and guidance. Together we learned even better ways to communicate and often enjoyed laughter! I joyfully remember that Friday when I bathed her and got her ready for her big day, as I referred to it. My plan was to see if she could walk to the front door and out onto the porch. I had hoped that earlier in our relationship. She was unhappy then. But now, she seemed to have more confidence and the motivation to be outdoors. I dressed her in her black pants and a yellow top that had a border of lace at the collar. I found a necklace that worked well with the outfit and slipped on a black cardigan sweater. I could tell that she was getting excited about her upcoming adventure. I asked her to stand at her walker, as usual, and we began walking toward the hallway together. One step at a time, she walked slowly and carefully through the hallway. As we passed by the kitchen the smell of homemade chicken soup rushed out at us. Ruth stood at the doorway smiling and clapping. Olive moaned a smile. We reached the front door and Ruth –

who was a partner in this plan from the beginning – opened it up to a beautiful, cloudless early spring day. It was warmer than the time of year called for and Olive was alighted with joy. She was beaming as I led her to a comfortable straight chair that Ruth and I carried out earlier that day. We were afraid that the rocker would be dangerous for her since her balance was no longer trustworthy.

Not wanting to tire her too much as she needed to walk back to her room, I told her it was time to go in after twenty minutes or so. I wanted very badly to see that she had a longer period of time out there and maybe dinner at the kitchen table, but I was frightened to ask that much of her then. Her energy and strength had declined so much and other than the range of motion exercises and my walking her three times a week, I did not think she could manage much more than she had already given.

Olive made it back to her room, sat in her chair and smiled. She held her hand out and grabbed my hand in thanks. I was so pleased and happy for her. It was a wonderful day! And a momentous week. Olive screamed and cried quite infrequently and when she did, a calm and reassuring voice quieted her. Ruth was scheduled to stay with her until late that evening and would be covering the weekend days as well. Harry and Nancy would resume their daytime care of her on Monday.

So at least, for the weekend, I did not worry about Olive. I enjoyed my weekend and planted spring onions that could go in early. My neighbor had me over for dinner Saturday evening. She was also a widow. Our husbands passed away in the same calendar year. Tough year. Other than sharing our love of rocking chairs and wine, we often got together at each other's homes for a meal and a few hours of Scrabble or a card game. The hostess would make the dinner and the guest would bring the dessert. We each had our favorites so it became a habit that she would bring a pecan pie when she was the guest, and I would take an apple cake with cream cheese frosting when she cooked. We would discuss family, friends, flowers, church, and other things in which we shared an interest. We also enjoyed adult beverages that would prompt us to giggle a lot after the second glass. Luckily, our houses were just a country block apart. How wonderful it is to have a friend to lighten your load, provide comfort and laugh with! We were both blessed.

Monday came too soon for me.

As I pulled up to the Cain's home that morning, I did not notice another car. I felt fear and then I told myself that Harry or Nancy probably ran to the store for something or had an errand to run. My visit was scheduled from eleven a.m. to one p.m. that day per their request. It would make sense that someone might be out.

As I was walking to the house, I heard a cry – no, a scream – a wail! I ran up the stairs to the door. It was locked. A haunting wail. I knocked and knocked on the door and called their names. Nancy! Harry! No answer. As my mind became louder than my emotions, I realized the noises were coming from outside of the house.

I ran as fast as a seventy-seven-year-old can around the side of the house where I thought I detected the wailing. There, in a chair – the one that she sat in on the front porch just three days before - in front of an old oak tree sat Olive. Screaming, crying, wailing all at one time. And both the chair and Olive were tied to that old oak tree! Such anger arose in me that I could never describe it. Who in the world would tie their mother to a tree so they wouldn't have to take care of her?

When Olive recognized who was coming toward her, her screaming stopped, but the crying continued. How do you stop something that was involuntarily started?

When I reached Olive, I stroked her head, hugged her, and did all I could to quiet her and assure her that she had been rescued. "Olive. I am here now, and we will get you away from here," I calmly told her. I had noticed the walker close to the tree which encouraged me. I was able to untie the rope that went around her waist, between the spindles on the chair back and around the tree. The knot was tight, but I managed to get it free and removed the rope from around her. I noticed the apron she had on was full of her breakfast – Cheerios and toast remnants and spots of milk. There were small pieces of bark on her lap as well.

I waited with her five or more minutes so that she might compose herself enough to walk to the house. It seemed like hours because I just wanted her to be happy and back in her bed! I talked with her and suggested that she could easily make it with my assistance. With the walker she was able to slowly move to the house. I held onto the back of her pants with one hand and dragged the chair with the other. I couldn't get into the house, so until I got Ruth with her key or the police, we would have to sit on the porch.

Thanking God with each step she was able to take, Olive and I both made the trek and sat comfortably on the porch. Olive had a certain look on her face – one of relief and appreciation. It was then that I noticed the birds were singing to us. Cardinals. I wondered if they sang to Olive as she sat under that tree, treated like a criminal.

"Marie," I said to myself, "get your act together. How will you get help if you can't get into the house to use the telephone?" I thought of breaking a window and climbing in. Then, I made sure Olive was OK and I walked around the house. Perhaps there was an open window or a door I had not noticed. To my dismay there was neither. I went back to the porch and sat down, patting Olive's hand to reassure her. I then heard a noise – "Oh, my goodness!" Here came Ruth's car and we were rescued.

That key couldn't turn fast enough for me. I felt like we had been running from the very outdoors themselves. Crazy the thoughts and emotions you have in such stressful circumstances. I knew that Olive must be exhausted, and I wanted to clean her up and get her into bed. Olive was washed, clothed, and sitting up in bed by the time Molly arrived. The VN pulled into the driveway just less than five minutes later.

Oh, how I had wished that Olive could tell her story that day! She revealed different expressions in reaction or response as the nurse and Molly spoke to her. Some expressions I had not before seen on that lovely, wrinkled face. They disturbed me and I wanted to know the truth and exactly what happened. Did Harry and Nancy get too much of a taste of their freedom from responsibility the week before? Did Olive scream and cry more than ever when she saw them that Monday morning? Who would know? Even if the two miserable relatives would describe the "event," they were certainly not to be trusted that they were telling the truth. "They tried a helpless human being outside to a tree" went continually through my mind. Looking at Olive's face made me angry at times and at others, I felt my own pain for her. Perhaps disgust is a word that I do not want to avoid using, either. Nancy and Harry disgusted me. Yes, they did.

MK arrived a bit later and the four of us – me, MK, the VN, and Molly excused ourselves from Olive's room and sat together at the kitchen table to determine our next moves. Ruth stayed behind to keep her Mom company. We were sure Olive did not want to be alone. There were dirty dishes in the sink and a toaster on the counter. Empty coffee cups also indicated that the two had enjoyed breakfast before they left the house. I wondered if they had the stomach to eat before or after they took Olive to the tree.

Needless to say, the police were called and two officers, a man and a woman, had arrived before Harry and Nancy pulled into the driveway. Their reactions to the police, the VN, Molly and MK were incredulous.

"Why are you here at our house?" blurted Nancy as they walked in. "Why are you here?" she distinctly asked the officers. "Has something happened to Olive?" she said in a voice with great innocence.

The two officers asked the rest of us to leave the room so they could freely speak to the pair. We went into Olive's room and stood – waiting to hear a verdict about these two. After a few minutes, the officers, Harry, and Nancy appeared and began walking to the front door, opened it and continued outside. The lady officer stopped to talk with us.

"We are escorting these two to the station for additional discussion. I do not know if they will or will not be back this evening. Is there someone that can stay with Olive until we are certain of her care?"

"I am happy to stay with Mom," Ruth responded. "She is safe

with me." MK offered to send me to help out on off days knowing that Lizzie would cover it with discretionary funds. She always produced something.

I am happy to end this story by telling you that Olive was placed in a nursing facility that was managed by a good director – one that cared for the people in her charge. Harry and Nancy were found guilty of the "crime." After they served their punishment – I never knew what that was – they left the area. I visited Olive weekly as a friend for about six months before she experienced a major stroke and passed away. I learned that Ruth was in her Mother's will as the owner of the house and property upon her death.

Lizzie

THE CHARACTER THAT WARMED HEARTS

"WHERE'S MY WAGON ON WHEELS?" Clara used to say when she phoned the office, talking with whoever happened to answer the phone. All the office staff knew her voice and the reason for her call automatically. She was receiving services from most of the Agency's programs, and they had all experienced "special" times with her aside from today's call. Some of the telephone calls were quite sobering, while some of them were very amusing and put a break in our day.

The tell-tale voice was high pitched and shaky, almost like the vibrato of a singing voice. It was also loud! Staff lovingly mimicked her because they all had at one time or another, been the one to answer the Clara call around noon. "Where's my wagon on wheels?" she would ask, clearly annoyed.

"It's coming, Clara," they would answer and then she would promptly hang up. She was, of course, talking about her meal delivery that was, according to her, late. Not always as sharp as a tack, Clara knew what time it was and when she was hungry. She happily never complained about the meal – only the time of delivery. Sometimes she called to speak with me specifically and I honestly loved it when I heard over the intercom, "Lizzie, Clara on the phone!"

One day MK paged me. "Angie is on the phone and wants to speak to you about Clara." I stopped working with Anna regarding some other client issues in her first-floor office and walked up the steps to take the call at my desk.

A few years before, an anonymous benefactor donated many thousands of dollars to the Agency each of three Christmases. The first gift was ninety thousand dollars, the second sixty thousand and the third thirty thousand. I was never told who this person was (I was sworn to secrecy each time before the check changed hands) but worked with his (or her) accountant to provide a plan for the utilization of the gifted money each year. Every year, I was told that the benefactor was not totally pleased with the plan, but I never received any guidance regarding what he (or she) was looking for. I wanted to have the financial resources to provide health insurance of some quantity to my staff, Home Health Aides and nutrition workers, but there was never an abundant, consistent cash stream from any source to validate the purchase. Basically, I could not give this priority benefit one year and remove it the next.

I had been in my position for ten years now and worked well with my board. Always wanting to provide more security for our entire team, we chose to give bonuses to the aides at the end of the fiscal year according to their average weekly hours of work. Aides were hourly employees. (Logistics and the low Medicaid rates made it fiscally impossible to hire full-time, although we had given it a chance one year. Our reimbursement from the hospital for Medicare services arrived within an acceptable time period but that was just fifty percent of our business. With the large rural county, too much payroll time was spent on travel, an activity that was not reimbursable. We chose to use our unrestricted funds, as we had them, to give reduced-rate services to our private clients who needed that assistance.) There were those aides, like Angie, who worked every case offered to her regardless of time, day, or location. A number of aides were "pickier" about where and when they worked. All of these people were so welcome and so important. No matter when and how much they worked, they were special people. I knew this and held them in my heart with profound respect and devotion.

In deliberations with the Board Finance Committee following the first year's gift from the anonymous benefactor, it seemed to us that the best use of the money would be to build a secure operating foundation for the Agency itself, that would guarantee meeting payrolls, etc. for years to come – even when Medicaid continued to lower payment rates each year and private foundations narrowed their gifting. The federal grants had also been slowly getting smaller although we could still count on a slightly diminished amount. There were always those times when Judy would let me know that the Medicaid payments were another month behind. Because of her hard fine-tuned work, we never a missed or made a late payroll throughout the years. Only once did we have to go to the local bank, who graciously gave us a short-term loan based on the Medicaid hours that had been billed but not yet paid. Cash flow for several reasons was always top of mind regarding operations.

And so, the plan for the use of the very gracious donation was to carefully look for a property that could be owned, eliminating the rental of office and training space, thereby deleting that line item in the budget that was shared with all of the valuable programs and services out of this one Agency. Finding the property to purchase was not an easy endeavor, but an old, two-story building was selected outside of the urban area. It worked well for a number of years.

"Clara, Clara," I talked to myself, probably smiling and rolling my eyes, as I sat in my desk chair and picked up the phone to talk to Angie. I always made myself available to the aides when it was not a medical or care issue that would first be transferred to a staff nurse, instead, and I enjoyed – or mostly enjoyed – the conversations I had with them. I knew so many of the team well that we could briefly catch up on their kids, needs for a new car or frig, the new puppy, and other things about their personal lives during a work call. Angie had called that day to tell me that she was growing increasingly worried about Clara and wondered if I would go to her home to assess the situation. I was a Licensed Social Worker in the State with years of experience in behavioral health before I took the Executive Director position at the Agency. "Sure, Angie. I can run out this week sometime. But do you want to be there when I come?" I thought it could give me a better idea of her concerns if I met her there.

Angie told me that wasn't necessary, that she just wanted another point of view on the situation. It had nothing to do with her state of health, but habits and living situations that were worrisome.

"OK, sure. Hopefully, I can help." I thought to myself, "Maybe I will have to get the department of social services to go in again." Our Agency frequently worked with the department on cases. It approved monies funneled by the State Department of Human Services to organizations that could provide services to county residents. Our Agency could never take a specific amount of money for granted, especially annual grants. The Director of this county department was especially difficult in dealings with me and other strong female leaders that received county funding. Those of us in this position got together over lunch once a month and talked on the phone often to find ways to avoid the problems with him and assure the funding was continued. We also had shoulders to cry on and the opportunity to complain, curse or whatever needed to happen to bring us down to earth emotionally following some type of conflict with him. He once accused me of lying during a public meeting. I was crazy angry but knew that nothing I would do to contradict him would help.

The social workers and my Agency often had mutual clients. We reached out to them for help with behavioral problems or situations that our aides encountered that required supplemental interventions to our routine care. Occasionally, the county provided additional payment for a swat team (a group of aides) to tackle the worse possible conditions found in a client's home. The assistant director of the department maintained a good relationship with me, so I felt comfortable asking for help when needed.

I had the opportunity to go to visit Clara later that week. I called first to tell her I was stopping by, and she apparently had no problem with that. "Yeah," she said and hung up the phone. As I drove the fifteen miles or so to her home, I wondered to myself what could possibly be the unsafe, worrisome situation that Angie talked about. If it were that bad, she certainly would have asked me to send someone right away. I turned up the sound on my car radio and was happy to hear a song that I could sing along with. "We'll see," I said aloud to myself and proceeded to sing to the "Piano Man." Thank goodness no one could hear me sing in the car. It was a usual practice for me.

The Department of Social Services had been dealing with Clara's general neediness and her "presence" in the community for some time. Clara would occasionally wander. Maybe once a month, her wandering would lead her to her local bank where she would have a seat in the lobby and refuse to leave. Clara would just sit there, talking to herself and others in her memorable voice. The bank, after an episode or two, learned to call her social worker, Andy, who would drive out, pick her up, and take her home.

Clara was thin, yet not what anyone could consider tiny. Her back and shoulders were broad and hunched over a bit, indicative of 90 years on this earth and a hard life. She wore stained and well-worn house dresses and old, cut off nylons pulled up to her knees with excess rolled under. Her shoes were terribly worn, with holes in the soles and missing stitching around the top. Clara walked quickly and with a purpose everywhere she went – even throughout her house. I always imagined she was a little short on intelligence but strong in her resolve to live this life with her head up! Her hair was white as snow, about chin length, straight, and wispy. With her walk, her hair fairly flew around her head – she was a cross between a cartoon character and an aged Scarlet O'Hara.

I had delivered her meals once, but only had gotten as far as the kitchen that day. This day was quite different.

Clara's house sat close to a uniquely narrow road which made parking there dangerous. I even hated to drive on that road – its incline was extremely steep and when you approached it at its highest peak, you could not see the road beyond it at all. It was like a roller coaster in that you had to move your car ahead into noth-ingness to meet the down slope. The move forward was a bit disconcerting even when you knew the road was there to catch you. The Meals on Wheels drivers wouldn't deliver here on days when the roads were bad. I completely understood. I approached the house and parked. When I carefully got out of the car, I walked into the backyard where I knew Clara answered her door for the Meals on Wheels drivers.

I knocked on the door. Clara came walking with her swift, determined steps to let me into the house. She wore an apron over her housedress. The apron was pretty, a brightly flowered print, and looked almost new. I thought perhaps an aide had given it to her.

"Come in, come in," Clara said as she hastily waved me inside. I stepped into the kitchen and recognized it from my previous delivery visit. A few dirty dishes in the sink. An old refrigerator that looked as though the door did not close completely. The linoleum on the floor was faded, cracked, and broken in places, leaving behind the black tarry look of the glue that was used years ago to lay it down. But in the old, faded, and dilapidated spaces of that kitchen, I could sense the life and intention of the old lady that moved around in it. I could also see what Angie had been doing. It was old and needed repair, but it looked clean.

I was motioned from the kitchen to sit in the living room like an old friend who had stopped for a visit. "Cuppa cafee?" Clara asked, speaking like a country girl with a slight rural twang. There was a stern but not angry look on that face that was full of wrinkles. But it led others to want to get to know what was behind it. It looked to me as if she had just washed her hair – white as snow yet fine as a baby's. I declined the coffee and asked her if we could just sit and talk for a few minutes.

I looked around when we walked into the room. I was amazed at what I saw, and incredibly sad. My mind almost made a list of what I was seeing; it was all so telling of the person I was visiting. "Intimate and touchingly beautiful. But, oh, so, sad. Even devastating," I thought.

Clara was talking as I walked by the couch, which was also her bed, apparently. The couch was obviously old. Its surface sagged and the color of the fabric was severely faded. There was a pillow with a clean case on it and a brightly crocheted afghan throw. I wondered if she had made that herself at an earlier time. It brightened up the dingy room.

Clara pointed to her couch and grumbled, "I can't sleep at night on that thing! Mices keep poking me through holes in the bottom. They wake me up! Darn things." She sat in a chair next to it and looked at me; a suggestion for me to sit as well. At that moment, I could not help myself. I walked over to the couch and lifted a cushion to see if there really were holes in the couch. Yes, there were several holes in it, although I did not see any evidence that mice had been there. Hopefully, it is a broken spring that is poking her, I thought to myself. "Clara, do you set traps or anything to catch the mice," I asked. I received a one-word response, "No."

I slowly eased myself into a chair on the other side of the room from Clara. I was not comfortable but wanted to be polite and friendly. Clara and I were both a few feet in front and to the side of a wood stove. I assumed that she used this for heating her home. One of Angie's worries, I guessed. Dangerous with a gal like Clara stoking it. A fire hazard to say the least. Then, out of the corner of my eye, I noticed the big pile of Styrofoam containers next to it.

"Clara, are you burning your empty Meals on Wheels containers?"

"Yep. Don't need no wood as often," she responded. "They burn good!"

"But, Clara, doesn't it smoke and smell up your living room?" I asked, now genuinely concerned. "And I am sure this isn't good for your stove." I was thinking of perhaps a sticky build-up inside the stovepipe.

"Maybe a little bit, but it don't bother me no more," was Clara's answer. I knew that I would take those containers away and somehow get some wood in there for Clara quickly. I wondered if this was what Angie was worried about, perhaps beside the fact that she was burning anything in that stove at all.

Looking around the whole room, I noticed a closed door with bright light coming through the bottom and onto the floor in front of it. I also realized that the room in which we sat was dark and damp. Very much so, in fact. The walls had not been painted in years and the heavy coating of smoke from the wood stove had turned them into a brownish yellow. The curtains were drawn with truly little daylight peeking through. "But what was behind the door that was allowing daylight to funnel in," I wondered.

"Your house looks big from the outside, Clara. Can I see what is over there?" I asked while pointing to the door with the light under it.

Clara got up and walked toward the closed door. She opened it to reveal a rather large entryway with light streaming through the window of the front door to the house. It was rather pretty in there. The wood was smooth and shining – a lovely dark maple shade. The walls were papered with a bold, flowered print. Opposite the door she just opened was another which led to the other side of the house. This place was a duplex! Why didn't I see that when I pulled up?

"Is the other side yours, too?" I asked. Clara muttered something and opened the other door. It was like a different world! The aged, dusty curtains were open to abundant sunlight. The furniture looked quite a bit newer probably through lack of use and decoratively, it all worked together. Baffling.

"Is this yours?" I asked again.

Clara answered with a "Yep," closed the door and walked into her gloomy living room.

"Why don't you live over there?" I asked as I followed her.

"Don't need to," was Clara's reply.

I followed her back into her side of the house and closed the entryway door behind me that led to the other world. I sat down again to visit a little more, in shock and confusion. Living there might brighten her days and change her attitude. Actually, as I was thinking that, I found that I could not really describe her attitude except possibly one of acceptance.

I was chatting with Clara and asking if she needed anything, what she did with her time, did she enjoy any hobbies? As I continued to glance around the room, I asked Clara about a picture that was hanging on the wall behind her couch.

"Is that your wedding picture"? I asked. The bride was lovely in her white gown and veil. The groom wore a dark suit and tie. Maybe taken in the late thirties, I thought.

Clara's answer came as a mighty surprise. "Naw." Her voice lowered a bit as she told me that the picture was of her husband and his second wife. "I knew her, too, so I got a picture. I guess he liked her better."

What to say? After a pause, I stood up. "Well, Clara, it has been nice visiting with you today. I'm glad I got to know you a bit more. I enjoyed our conversation. I will take all these containers with me. The fumes are not good for you, and I am afraid they are doing something to your stovepipe which might start a fire. Do you have wood you can use tonight until I get some help for you? "

Clara told me that she had wood. She did not argue or complain about losing the containers. As I was walking toward the backdoor, I checked the refrigerator to make sure it was cold and there was no rotten food in it. It seemed fine. Angie was taking good care of her.

It took me a few trips to the car to gather all of the containers in it. With the last two containers tucked under my arm, I said goodbye to Clara with a smile. I wanted to hug and tell her I was sorry for her life situation and story, although I really didn't know that much about it – just those bits and pieces. I was so glad that Angie had asked me to go to see her. If nothing more, it probably spared Clara a lung disease or house fire from the Styrofoam pack-ages. I would ask social services to see about a replacement couch or cushions for it.

I had a solemn and thought-filled ride back to the office. No singing. I could always see her walking through the kitchen in my mind's eye when I thought of her. And her phone calls continued on and on. She is never to be forgotten by many people whose lives she unknowingly touched. I still get mad when I think of her husband.

Lizzie

PROFILES AND SHORT STORIES

WHEN I ARRIVED at the in-service, it was already a busy, noisy place with lots of laughter. I noticed Patty in the back of the room talking with MJ. I thought they must be discussing the new housekeeping client that had been assigned to Patty. They were going to announce the launch of the new housekeeping program tonight. MJ would have the opportunity to present it to the group before the speaker began. Such a new program, I was ashamed that I did not know more about its apparent first job. Note to self...

Ethel was there. I was so glad to see her. She was a special person. Ethel was a short, sweet, and beautiful elderly lady. Countless people in the county knew her and her late husband who had been the local barber. Talking with Ethel always revealed something new about her or a sick neighbor, someone's granddaughter or someone's trouble with their dog. She knew it all mainly because everyone loved her and trusted her with the inside of their lives. Ethel was also known for her writing. She spent hours each day writing letters to someone to cheer them up, wish them good health, celebrate a birthday or just to send a note that she was thinking of them. Ethel had been with the Agency for more than twenty years. Once an excellent aide, she was then doing mostly respite work. She was truly a joy and an excellent representative of our Agency. I worried about her sometimes. Like many of our clients, she was aging and all alone.

I noticed that Ethel and Gladys were chatting. I didn't believe they had any mutual clients, but both were longtime county residents and perhaps had mutual friends or acquaintances. Gladys worked in a town along the State border. She only had one client, but she was the most needed aide we had at that time. Her client, Hilda, lived alone on a second-floor walk-up. She was confined to her bed and was incontinent. Imagine! God forbid if there was a fire – she would never get out. Gladys walked the steps to take care of her morning, noon, and night. She got her up, washed her, diaper changed, fed her breakfast, and left water and a sandwich for her lunch before she left. If Gladys was somehow delayed from her noon visit, Hilda had something to eat until she arrived. If Gladys was prompt with that visit, Hilda enjoyed her sandwich, as Gladys did the laundry – at least washed it, then changed the patient and made her comfortable. Gladys always allowed the time for range of motion exercises with Hilda. Not that Hilda was going to run a marathon or even walk to the kitchen, but it worked her heart and muscles which were helpful to her good health. A snack was left at the bedside. At dinner time, Gladys would finish the laundry, go to the store or other errands, prepare, and serve dinner and got Hilda ready for bed. Fresh water was always left behind on the table next to the bed aside the phone. The 911 number and Hilda's address and phone number in bold, large writing were on a tablet next to the phone. Gladys cared for Hilda in this manner seven days a week. She rarely asked for a substitute and when she did, she spoke to them first to give them instructions! There was such a connection there. I never learned anything about Gladys' private life. MK knew more about her.

Just as I was turning from watching Gladys and Ethel talking, I felt an arm around me. Ginny, another terrific and responsible aide had come to see me. "Lizzie, did you hear what happened to me today?" she asked. I was a little taken back that something unusual or startling had happened that I had not known.

"No. What?"

Ginny continued. "I went to visit Mrs. Conlon this morning as usual. The door is always unlocked for me, so I walked in and called her name, so she knew that the "visitor" was me. "Ginny, come here quickly. I need you!" she called out in a shaky, almost frantic tone. I ran into her room not certain of what I would find. Was she having a heart attack? Diarrhea? What? Before I got to the opened bedroom door, I could smell a nauseating odor and heard soft squeaky sounds. Was she overrun by mice? Oh, my God. What?"

"Mrs. Conlon was lying on her bed in the same position, I imagined, that she had slept in. I knew from what I saw she wasn't going to move. The bottom of her bed was covered with blood and placenta. The mother cat was still cleaning the placenta off of her tiny kittens that were searching for their milk. They were making squeaking sounds. Have you ever seen new baby kittens? I counted six with their eyes closed, barely able to move, shivering and swiveling their little heads left and right for the scent of breakfast. They were adorable and the mother cat seemed quite comfortable and capable of taking care of her kids. Mrs. Conlon was emotional but not mad, nor happy. Still just surprised! Think about it. She told me she slept through the delivery!"

During this story I was both horrified at the beginning when the bed was full of blood, interested as the placenta part of the story came around, smiling at the knowledge of the momentous event and laughing at the entire scenario. Ginny also laughed as she continued the story of the process of moving the family to a box she prepared with old towels. Mrs. Conlon, she said, was smiling with pride as she watched the family in their new home. Removing the linens for laundering and getting Mrs. Conlon ready for her day was basically routine but the entire morning visit was certainly one for the story books.

"Are you going to take one of the kittens when they are weaned?" I asked Ginny.

"Yes, I think I am. After all, I will be their caregiver when I am there," she smiled. As Ginny walked away to get a drink of tea and find her seat, I noticed the time had whizzed by.

The chatter and laughter continued well past seven that evening, but no one seemed to care. Our speaker was a Board member, Martha Cole, who worked for the Department of Human Services, reporting to the County Human Services Director, and she was chatting it up as well. Martha had become a good friend of mine.

Those on our Board were terrific people. They were very responsive to me when I asked for additional business attention and supported me with the major decisions that I had to make. Two of our board members also ran a consignment shop for organizational funding. They did a phenomenal job and were kindly strict with their rules. Only clean, in-season and "wanted" clothing was accepted. It was very successful thanks to these two and many others that volunteered to keep the shop open Thursdays through Saturdays each week. They netted and donated to the organization a very sizable amount each year.

The presentation that evening was about Alzheimer's and how to help the spouse or caregiver cope with it. Martha's father had suffered from the disease and she and her mother cared for him for years. The stories she told the group that evening were helpful and provided therapeutic ways to assist in the situation. Her mother had gone to great lengths to prevent the times of anxiety that would change her husband's behavior with the flip of a switch. He was a sundowner, and the anxiety often overwhelmed him in the middle of the night. They put locks at the top of the doors to the outside and the basement where he would not look, nor could he reach. Because he urinated anywhere, they tore up all of the carpeting and laid linoleum so that the urine could be quickly cleaned up and there was no stain or odor. As a successful professional in a rather large company, her father insisted he had to go to work frequently and became belligerent if he could not go. Martha or her mom would help him into the front seat of the car telling him they were driving to work. Around the corner or perhaps a mile they would travel. This would settle him, and he would forget about going to work. They'd then drive home. These simple things eliminated anxiety for both parties. No longer infrequently, the Agency cared for Alzheimer's patients and useful tips, or sorrowful stories were often shared by the aides. The information from Martha that evening was interesting and very educational. We thanked her with a round of applause and then all started to make their way to the door for supplies and to say personal goodbyes.

Donna came up to me while others were chatting as they were leaving. "Hi, Lizzie" she said. "Do you have a minute to hear an Alzheimer's story from me?" she asked. "Something that happened to me yesterday. I wanted to tell it during the presentation tonight, but it would have interrupted Martha. Perhaps you can use it as you give presentations about the Agency and our work with Alzheimer's patients."

"Sure. Let's sit down so we don't clog the doorway. I want to hear about it."

Donna was one of our middle-aged aides who was a stay-at-home mom while her children were growing up. Two of the three kids were in high school and one in middle school at the time. When she realized that she wasn't needed at home to supervise or perform as a chauffeur, she signed up for our training class and had enjoyed the job since that time. She was dependable and efficient with a calm and caring nature. Of course, the staff loved her.

"I went to see Mrs. Benton yesterday according to our normal schedule. I go on Mondays, Wednesdays, and Fridays at 1:00 p.m. Yesterday when I walked in, I heard a noise like a sniffle and several words which I couldn't make out, and then I thought I heard crying. The sounds were coming from her dining room, so I walked that way. What I saw from the doorway was heart-wrenching. Standing at the sightline from one end of the dining table to the top of it, I saw Alice sitting in the chair at the far end from me. My eyes saw tears, sadness, tiredness, frustration, confusion, and self-pity. The table was laid with a linen tablecloth with six plates in addition to the one before Alice. The plates were appropriately accompanied by linen napkins folded in triangles and the needed silverware for a meal that included a salad and dessert. At the top left of each place setting was a lovely water glass. And in the middle of the tabletop were bowls and platters of food, long ago cooked and dished up for serving to her guests. It looked like a Thanksgiving dinner with turkey that was spoiled (you could easily tell), potatoes, green beans, stuffing, and gravy (with a noticeably thick skim on top). There was also a salad that was wilted and on the side table, I noticed a pie. Alice looked up at me with an angry face this time and shared her anger. "They come for Sunday dinner every week and they are not eating anything. Why?" She turned her head. "Why aren't you eating? I made all of your favorite food and you won't eat it," she yelled as she looked at the wall.

"Lizzie, I then realized who she was mad at. She was talking and yelling at the pictures of her family that hung on the wall by the table."

I immediately felt tears welling in my eyes and noticed the same on Donna's face. "Oh, my, no!" I said. "How sad. Oh, my God. How did you handle it?"

"I collected myself quickly and went to give her comfort. I didn't know what else to do at the time. It was an automatic reaction. The poor woman's eyes were red from crying. Her nose was dripping, and she pulled up the skirt on her dress to wipe it dry. So sad. I just put my arms around her and hugged her, talking quietly about the beautiful day outside. While my arms were still around her, I could feel her anger subside as I slowly walked her out of the room. I knew I had to change the topic and get her somewhere where she couldn't see those faces on the wall or the uneaten food on the table. She sat down comfortably on the couch, and I told her that since it was Monday, I would help her take a shower and fix her hair. I also suggested that she might want to lay down on the bed for a nap while I put something together for her dinner. I needed to have the time to privately clear the table and dispose of the spoiled food. Gratefully, she agreed to the plan. After bathing, she was able to sleep well - according to the snoring - for about forty-five minutes while I cleaned up the heartbreaking scene in the dining room. Lizzie, does her family come for Sunday every week? Do you know?" she asked me.

"No, I am unaware," I answered. "But I will ask MK and Anna tomorrow at the office and try to get some time with Martha tonight. If not, I will call her tomorrow. I am uncomfortable that she is living alone. Certainly, someone who can help with the situation needs to be aware of her mental status." We ended the conversation that evening but the next morning I did talk to Martha and placed a phone call to family members who were listed as an emergency contact. I also phoned Donna later that day to check and to thank and praise her for her insightful and compassionate work on Monday.

In-services were always interesting because the group personality and "mood" determined the mixture of laughter and the seriousness of business that evening. Most times it was a fairly even percentage of each. But always the fun and comfort of seeing each other and sharing the news somehow made the sad stories fade a bit.

MJ, Patty, Jane, and Ginny

WE NEED A TEAM!

LIZZIE ASKED me one day to start a small program dedicated to housekeeping only. There were always several aides who preferred the household duties over personal care. And some of our clients legitimately needed services to keep their homes clean. Housekeeping duties would also include errands and laundry if requested.

I was happy to do this for the Agency and knew of aides that would gladly do the jobs. I developed a handful of policies that were somewhat different from the aide policies but maintained the core of the operational guidelines they, as aides, always followed. One primary policy was if the client needed any type of personal care, the housekeeper – although a Certified Aide - was not to provide that type of service during that visit.

A friend of the Agency phoned one day soon after the program could be "a go" and asked to have housekeeping services delivered to his aunt who lived in an old farmhouse not far from the Agency's office building. Because this program had just been developed, MK offered to go on the first visit with me to meet with our client, Helen Short, and develop a work plan according to need and the number of visits we felt would be required. We hadn't yet developed a form to use for our files so this visit would also serve to outline the details of the client record.

As I drove up the lane to the house, I noticed MK's car was already parked, and she was sitting inside her vehicle waiting for me. The house and the grounds were both sorely uncared for. I was surprised by what I saw: scattered car parts; broken garden tools apparently left just where they became unusable; two curled up old hoses that were unattached to an outdoor faucet; a clothesline which was the color of rust swaying in the wind; and an old doghouse that had seen better days. It was empty with no hint of a dog around. The grass was long here and there but was otherwise barely surviving in churned up and muddy ground following heavy rains. MK and I were fortunate to find places to park without having to worry about pulling out again.

MK got out of her car and greeted me. We talked briefly about our surroundings and what we needed to accomplish inside. The clapboard farmhouse was like those we often ran into because the house and the resident, as well, needed help. The white paint was peeling everywhere, and the window frames appeared to be rotten in areas. As the two of us climbed the stairs, we were happy to note that they seemed safe despite the home's condition elsewhere.

MK knocked on the door. A short, stocky man opened the door and welcomed us inside. He introduced himself as Helen's son, Bill. Helen then walked out of another room which appeared to be the kitchen from our angle. She was using her walker carefully and slowly, but with a confident step. I was pleased to see that. The first thing you noticed about Helen herself was the powder puff of white, curly hair on her head. Her small features complimented the puff perfectly. A woman of seventy-eight years, she wore a printed housedress that looked well-loved. Her body was trim and despite age, and medical concerns, her posture was quite straight, even as she leaned over the walker to grab the bars.

"Hello," she chimed in a small voice. "I am so happy to meet you." Her smile was distinct. "I am Helen Short. I see you have met my son, Bill. He is my eldest. His two brothers also live here with me." Again, a smile from one that was proud of what she just told us - three sons living with her.

When we spoke on the way up to the house, MK and I agreed that the boys were probably caring for her, especially with the cleaning and laundry needs around the house. But as we looked at each other just then, we shared a glance that maybe it was the other way around? Bill had not, as yet, said a word to us since he introduced himself. And Helen was very perky!

Helen suggested we sit and talk in the kitchen, so we followed her into the room and found seats around the round – and dirty – kitchen table. My job was to ask questions about their needs, what supplies and equipment they had with which to clean and do laundry and other inquiries about how to do our job in their home that worked with their timing and lifestyle. MK had more general administrative experience and asked questions to assure the client record had all of the necessary information. The healthcare field is overflowing with regulations regarding not just practice, but also related to payment. Lizzie wanted everything done properly including necessary details. The quality of our services, and also the Agency's liability was always on Lizzie's mind.

The kitchen was a mess –one of the worst I had seen in a while. Dirty dishes were not just in the sink but stacked on the countertop as well. With the condition of the outside of the house, noticing the broken linoleum floor was not a shock. A large pot with drips of something that had boiled over was on the stove. And on the floor in the corners by the refrigerator and the counter by the sink, mousetraps were set with dried up cheese. The table had clearly been used for dining and small remnants of food were here and there. Helen smiled as she answered our questions and just chatted. I began wondering at times if Helen was mentally "with us." I reminded myself that the request for service came from her nephew who was a notable professional in the community. Still her son Bill said nothing but sat quietly with us as we gathered information and learned – from Helen – of her needs.

Helen said she needed someone to take care of them, especially her boys. She asked if she made a list, could the aide go to the store for her? And how about our laundry, she added. MK inquired why her sons could not do their laundry or go to the store?

Helen giggled and in her soft little voice said, "Oh, my no. I had the boys go to the store for me once or twice, but they never came home with all of the items on my list. And they missed the most important ones like milk, bread, and coffee. We had plenty of cookies and cakes, though," she laughed again. "Oh, those boys!"

The picture was coming together a bit now. I thought I would give Bill a chance to change the story, so I asked him if he would like to give me a tour of the house and answer my questions while MK and Helen finished the other types of questions.

"OK," he said and got up from his chair. As he walked to another room, I followed, anxious to see the conditions that we would find in the bathrooms and bedrooms, and also to hear from Bill.

"This is the living room," Bill said as we just peeked inside. "Nothing important there. A TV and chairs." And he was right. That was about it. But several chairs made me think that the family might sit together to watch a show or two.

Back out into the hall, we walked toward a hall closet and an open door that I thought might be a bathroom. "Is that a linen closet, Bill?" I asked. He looked at me with a questioning expression. "I mean, is that where you keep the towels and sheets? Do you have enough towels for the family so that clean ones are always available?"

"Oh, yeah," he answered. He opened the closet door just enough that I could see perhaps five or six assorted sheets and one or two towels.

"Are there more towels?" I asked him.

Bill swiftly went to the bathroom, swung the door closed a bit, and grabbed a towel off of a hook on the back of the door. "Here is the towel that we use," he told me frankly and without any type of emotion on his face. "We get a clean one on Mondays."

Now, I simply continued our tour. I was dumbstruck. One

towel. Four people. How many uses a week? Before walking away from the bathroom, I peeked inside it and merely shuddered at the insides of the tub and sink. Thank goodness, I did not go in and lift up the toilet lid.

"Where are your brothers today, Bill?" I asked as we walked down the hall a bit more.

"I guess they're upstairs in their rooms," he answered. "Our bedrooms are upstairs. Mom is the only one that sleeps down here. Her room is straight ahead."

Helen's room was quite nice. She apparently had herself together enough to keep her space at least tidy. The bedspread was old, but a nice light blue with yellow and pink flowers. The bed appeared to be queen-sized. She had two dressers, one with a mirror. There were an assortment of knickknacks and a piece or two of jewelry on top of one. The other had a doily cover with two music boxes atop it. "How sweet! Did you and your brothers give your mom the music boxes?" I inquired of Bill who still had no appetite for conversation.

"No," was his answer. "I think my father did. They are kind of old."

I thought about going upstairs to see the other bedrooms and meet the brothers. But as I walked toward the kitchen again, I heard male voices intermingled with MK's and Helen's. "Thank God," I said to myself. I really did not want to venture up there today. Our job would be sufficient downstairs for the first visit or so. The housekeeper can cross the upstairs bridge. My main goal at the time was to see that Helen had clean quarters overall. Of course, that would include spaces the boys also used, but she was the client. And a sweet one at that!

I met Arnie and Caleb in the kitchen. They had pulled up chairs at the table. The four people were engaged in enjoyable conversation regarding the history of the house and the property. The boys – all three, actually – had animation in their faces as they recalled their youth and the good times that the whole family had on the farm when their grandparents and their dad were alive. Caleb was obviously the youngest according to the stories they told that day. He was apparently quite the scamp. Helen beamed as they reclaimed their fond memories as youngsters on the farm. She was so calm and innocent in her smile and manner. Despite the mess, she was happy!

After fifteen minutes or so of listening to their childhood stories, MK and I excused ourselves and said our goodbyes to the four. When outside, we agreed to meet in the office first thing the next morning to discuss our "findings" and the schedule I would propose to Helen.

"I think I will suggest two three-hour visits the first week, two two-hour visits the second week, and one two-hour visit per week after that," I said to MK that morning. "I am thinking that we will not do the upstairs, yet if she is paying for our time, maybe we should. It is housekeeping, after all, and not home care. Maybe we should clean the whole place? Shall I check with Lizzie? Whatever the decision, it will be one for the housekeeping program policies."

MK looked at me with a nod and I immediately went upstairs to hopefully grab Lizzie's attention and get her response right away. Lizzie was at her desk on the phone. However, she held up her just-a-minute finger and I waited until she was able to get off of the call.

"What's up? How did yesterday's visit go at Mrs. Short's house?" I rolled out the visit scenario and came right to the point. Not an extremely complicated issue, really.

"With the new housekeeping program, will we still only serve the client if others in the household can fend for themselves, or do we service the whole family?" I posed to Lizzie.

She didn't have to think long and told me that we would do the whole house if, in fact, that was what the client was willing to purchase. Otherwise, the job could be negotiated. That made perfect sense to me – a bit difficult after working with respect to the aide regulations for so many years. I started with the Agency as an aide and loved the work. After about three years, though, I needed a new challenge and applied for the job as Director of the Respite

Care program which required the service of certified aides. I basically lived those regulations and policies.

I informed MK of the decision. We then discussed her client record interview with Helen. Together we scoped out the housekeeping client application and file record. Later, I put everything together in a professional manner for immediate use. I also would see that the entire staff became familiar with it and report that the program was "live" at the upcoming in-service. Lizzie had already determined the rates.

I upped the schedule that I originally proposed by adding an hour to each step-down of required service. Thus, we opened our first housekeeping client by providing three three-hour visits in the first week. I assigned Patty, who was a competent, kind, and caring aide and had requested an additional two or three housekeeping hours per week. I thought she would serve the Short household well with her kindness and terrific work ethic.

I spoke to Patty following her first visit. She, too, had been surprised at the indoor condition of the house but told me that she had seen worse. It was only a normal mess that had been ignored for too long. The kitchen dishes, counters, and cabinet door fronts cleaned up all right. The floor, she mentioned, was difficult to mop because of the torn and missing linoleum. Helen's bedroom needed dusting and vacuuming. Patty laundered the sheets and dirty clothing she found in a basket in the closet. She had not yet tackled the bathroom, she told me. She felt that might be a job for an entire shift. Luckily, she had located a stack of bath towels in a closet. She would wash them the following day when she intended to clean the bathroom and perhaps start upstairs.

After Patty's third three-hour visit that week, we connected again on the phone.

"Well, I made a good dent in that place, MJ. After completing what would be a normal routine cleaning of the downstairs, I ventured up the stairs to the second floor. There are three bedrooms up there and one bathroom. You could tell three men live up there," she giggled. "There were dirty – really dirty - and smelly clothes that I had to throw in the washer almost immediately. I washed the linens and the two towels that the boys had used in the bathroom and remade the beds. I will go to Goodwill and get more towels for this house. Both kitchen and bath." This time, not much of a giggle as a sigh came over the telephone wires to me.

"Frankly, I am happy to be here despite the mess and odors upstairs. Helen is so delightful and funny! While I was downstairs working, we talked. She told me about her life, her husband, how she wished she could work outside on the farm again and how she missed the cows and goats they once had. Her sense of humor is sharp – sometimes self-deprecating to make us both laugh. How she loves and spoils her boys. I don't believe she knows they are men and rather helpless ones at that."

"Do you think Helen is 'with-it' all the time?" I asked Patty.

"I have noticed that she is not always engaged with time and her environment. She is not generally 'lost' for lengthy periods of time, but I have become concerned that there is much she doesn't seem to be aware of," she responded.

"Is there a kitchen accident to be worried about?" I asked. The aides frequently have to request that knobs be removed from stoves by the family or social worker to prevent the pots that are forgotten, then cook dry, and start fires.

Patty told me she wasn't concerned now but would keep it in mind.

The schedule and the job worked well and went smoothly for two months or so.

I stopped by once or twice just to say hello and check in. Things seemed fine, as Patty told me. Helen did seem a sweetheart and was rather funny. She wore a dress with an apron over it one day that reminded me of a dear aged grandmother that would be portrayed in an old Hollywood movie. And that beautiful white hair really topped the role off! This was one of my drop-in visits that helped me through an otherwise stressful day. Helen did me a favor!

I was first in the office one morning and ran from the building's door to pick up an early phone call. Helen's son, Arnie, was crying softly as he told me that Helen had succumbed to a heart attack after being admitted to the hospital the night before. I was immediately saddened because all of us had become so fond of her, her silly laugh (a giggle, really), her infectious cheerful outlook, and simply her overall love of life and family. I knew I would always remember that white curly head of hair. I knew the boys would be devastated and I worried about them. Were they really unable to care for themselves or just lazy because someone else was always willing to do it for them?

I called Patty to let her know about Helen. She was shocked and tears came easily with the news. I asked if she wanted to ask the boys about plans for a service or if she preferred that I do it. We ended the conversation in agreement that I would speak to her nephew since I knew him. That particular day was not scheduled for a housekeeping visit, so I decided to give him time without outside concerns and would phone him the following afternoon.

That conversation with her nephew went well. He informed me of the funeral plans. We spoke briefly about the housekeeping service. At the time, however, he decided to stop the service thinking that the boys needed to stand up to the plate. They were grown men, after all! I agreed – but doubted it would happen.

I saw the boys at Helen's funeral. I wanted to attend the service to pay my respects to that sweet lady and to talk with her sons, although briefly. Bill, Arnie, and Caleb stood solemnly side by side at the casket and appropriately interacted with those others that came to say goodbye to Helen. They had cleaned themselves up for the occasion.

I spoke to Patty who was able to change her schedule a bit to attend the funeral and say her goodbyes to Helen.

Patty phoned me the next day to talk and share her emotional response of the day before. "When I heard the news, I was incredibly sad, she told me as we began the conversation. I have lost other clients before – more than several - but this one hurt a bit more than others. I could see her walking through the kitchen in my mind's eye. She had such a presence of happiness, fun, and love."

She shared a bit more information with me that was personal. But I was happy to listen. She told me that Chet helped her through her sadness of losing Helen. Luckily, he wasn't sorry that she had taken that extra housekeeping work. She closed her end of the conversation by saying that life was good, and she was thankful for God's blessings. I responded in a way to acknowledge her sadness at the loss and thanked her for her wonderful work.

Despite Lizzie's talk with Helen's nephew regarding the ending of the service we had been performing prior to Helen's death, the time came for Patty's return to the Short's home...

Chet answered the phone the morning MJ called. I was putting things together in a Crockpot for our dinner that night. Generally speaking, a call at that time of day required his response. Chet is a sales representative for a food distributor and there are those days when deliveries go awry, or unhappy clients call the central office and ask for him. The system was set up to transfer calls directly to our phone number given the correct office extension.

"Hello," I heard his voice from the kitchen.

"Hi, MJ… How are you?…Yes, she's here…Just a minute…Patty, phone for you!"

I plugged in the Crockpot, set it on low, and went to take the call.

"Hi, MJ. How are you?" I greeted her with a smile on my face that she could not see but I hope she heard.

"Hi Patty. I'm good." She continued. "We got a Medicare referral this morning - two times three – for Bill Short. He had a mild heart attack, and they are sending him home. Anna asked me to give you a call since the scheduler is going crazy with changes this morning. We wondered if you would take it. I know you don't really want more work, but I thought because you know the client and the home – and remember it will probably only be one or two weeks – you might accept it. They would like it to start today if you can. Of course, the VN will meet you there.

We can adjust the time of day for future visits if it works best for you."

"Sure" I said and provided a time when I would arrive so that they could inform the hospital when the VN should be there. MJ was pleased and I was curious to see the boys and how things were going. I was glad that Bill's heart attack was not so bad.

"I am so happy to have taken care of that situation," I said to myself after Patty and I ended that conversation. Now, I had other work to do beside respite and housekeeping services. The team kept me busy and because I understood every facet of the inner office workings, other staff felt free to ask me to pitch in and help with whatever they could not manage at the time.

The next morning as I was reviewing last-minute notes to myself from the day before and on a call that I should have placed the day before as well, my phone rang. I ended my conversation quickly and answered the ring. "Hi, MJ. This is Patty."

"Hi, Patty," I said with enthusiasm. "How's Bill doing?"

"Oh, my God, MJ. You should see the house! The kitchen was a mess – worse than it was the first time we walked into it! But upstairs...." At this, Patty's voice was shaking, and I thought she was crying. "The smell upstairs! On my God, MJ. Bill is urinating and defecating in buckets and empty coffee cans, all left up against the wall in his room. The bathroom is similar because the toilet is clogged with brown toilet paper and no one has tried to unclog it, apparently! Oh my God! I have never seen – or smelled – anything like this. I was retching the whole time I was there. I need help!"

I wanted to gag myself. "OK. Patty, I will get help for you as quickly as I can!"

She sighed and said "Thanks. I am home, taking a shower now, and pouring myself a big glass of wine!" and then hung up.

I went to the nurses' office right away, hoping at least one of them were there. Jackpot! They were both at their desk. "Ladies, do I have a favor to ask of you!" I announced as I found an extra chair and sat down to face both as they swiveled from their desk to acknowledge me. I proceeded to tell them the Short family story.

Both were wide-eyed and, for a brief time, speechless. "Oh, my God," said Anna. It certainly seemed to be the phrase of the afternoon. I try not to say that, but rather, "Oh my goodness!" But right now, the situation seemed worthy of His attention.

"How do we get help for Patty – like a cleaning swat team? Does Lizzie have that kind of money to pay for the time that is necessary for more than one person to tackle the mess?" Anna and MK looked at each other for a moment and then MK picked up the phone to call Lizzie who was still in the office. She held the phone out so we could all hear the exchange.

It was quickly decided that Lizzie would call Social Services the next day to ask for emergency money for the mission. Whether or not they could produce financing in any amount, the agencies together would work it out. She suggested two other aides be assigned to help Patty. "Thanks, Lizzie," I said loudly so she could hear.

"No problem!" was her reply before she hung up.

After a few aide names were shared among us, we unanimously decided to ask Jane and Ginny to help Patty. I agreed to make those calls the first thing the next morning to find mutually acceptable times and days for the three of them to start the job. (Oh, God, please let them say "Yes"!) The Agency would take their advice on service frequency after they assessed the project. I mentioned we would have to provide cleaning supplies. A plea went out immediately over our office intercom and the next day everyone pitched in to loan or purchase what was needed. I bought each of the aides heavy rubber gloves to add to the donations or things borrowed.

A big sigh emanated from me the following morning when I received the two "yeses" needed from Jane and Ginny. Together we easily fixed the day and time of the first team visit, which was that afternoon. Ginny did not live too far from the office, and she picked up the loaned and donated buckets, mops, cleaning fluids, paper towels, garbage bags and a box of latex gloves that the aides routinely used.

Lizzie talked to Social Services who said they would find the money to pay a single invoice from us if the time charged was line itemed per individual worker. Lizzie also phoned the VN to notify her and spoke to the boys' uncle. That conversation, Lizzie said, was quite difficult but she was honest with him. She felt bad for him – he would obviously have responsibilities ahead that wouldn't be easily met. As always, our crew attacked the pressing need that was presented to them quickly and began meeting the challenge the very next day. Our troops were good people and anxious to help in any and all situations. Doing so, we also smiled, laughed, and enjoyed each other. I always found that amazing.

There was one upside to this current Short family health crisis. All three "housekeepers" were Certified Aides. The VN could go over the care plan with all of them and whoever chose or had the opportunity to provide the homecare to Bill could give it. Medicare regulations would be fulfilled. Whoever would provide the care would have to do so either before or following the cleaning of the day although it was immediately clear that the trio would have to clean Bill's room first before anyone could provide clean, safe, and loving personal care in that environment.

I met Patty, Jane, and Ginny there that afternoon to survey the situation and be of help to them. Patty wasn't even close to exaggeration when she described the scene and its odor on the phone to me. I got on the phone and asked Anna to bring some hospital masks to us as we tackled Bill's room.

Bill greeted us from his bed as we walked through his bedroom door. "Ladies. Hi, Patty."

Near the nightstand was a table with a tray. The tray held a cup and an empty plate. One of his brothers must have brought him breakfast. I thought to myself, "How could he possibly eat in here?" The trio and I huddled together and decided to rid the room of the human waste and wash the immediate environment around the vessels that held it. We would have to get on our hands and knees to do so – cleaning the wall directly above the floor, the molding, and floor. I was sorry I hadn't thought of bringing a fan, but I did have a bottle of Lysol which at least told our noses that there was a clean surface somewhere.

"Thank goodness I was not alone to take care of this mess," Patty told me. "I was also grateful that the Agency provided heavy rubber gloves in addition to the latex for us to use. Just picking up a coffee can or a bucket made one swallow hard in toleration of the smell. Just imagine if you had to touch them bare-handed."

The Agency had also provided heavy-duty black garbage bags. Coffee can after coffee can filled with solid voided product had been dropped into the bags. We were careful not to overload them. It seemed disgusting to dispose of it that way. At least we could dispose of the urine because Ginny was able to unclog the toilet after twenty minutes of using the plunger. Ginny is a small, thin lady who surprised herself that she could continue the difficult plunge after plunge until the roadblock was gone. I thought of Chet who could have gotten it done so much more quickly. But knowing him, he would have gagged from upstairs all the way down the stairs and into the front yard!

The human waste was gone, and Jane and Ginny were cleaning all around the area with the Lysol water. The odor was at least diminishing somewhat. Patty and I talked in the hallway about the next reasonable task to undertake with just thirty minutes left of our first cleaning day there. The hallway needed to be vacuumed and cleaned, but there would be quite a lot of foot traffic in that area before we had sufficiently completed our job. After watching the plunging, we were all aware the bathroom would be a time-consuming task to be taken up the next time.

We began looking for clean linens that could be used until those currently on the beds and in the bathroom could be washed. Did Bill have any clean clothes or underwear that the one of us who did his personal care could use after washing him up? He needed to be washed, dressed and up out of bed as soon as we arrived. We could do that at the next visit without worry. We continued our search for the needed clean items.

As our discussions continued, we heard a voice from downstairs. It was the VN. I ran down the steps to greet her. She had not been to this house before and was staring open-mouthed at the disgrace of the kitchen and first floor in general. She was apparently new to the Visiting Nurses organization and was a lovely looking young lady.

"Hi. I'm Linda. I suppose you are from the Agency?" she asked.

"Yes. You can call me MJ for now." I answered. "Has anyone filled you in about the job we have here? Luckily for us, we are all Aides and can work with you, per your normal system. Right now, we are the cleaning swat team, just finishing up our allotted hours for the day. Your patient has not yet had his personal care because we had to clean the room first for safety's sake."

I proceeded to enlighten her of the situation and what we had accomplished that day. She looked startled. She took my arm and said, "You must be angels. Let's go up so I can meet Bill and see what can be done from my end." So up the stairs we went. I caught Linda putting her hand over her nose and mouth several times. I was aware, however, that just two hours before it had been much worse. I noted that quietly under my breath as we climbed.

Linda and I ran into Patty in the hallway as she walked out of the room with used towels and rags in her arms. She continued to take the dirty linens downstairs to the washer while Linda and I walked into the room. Jane and Ginny lifted their heads from their work of continuing to clean wall and floor surfaces by hand when Linda and I walked in. We also planned to mop the floor. The hand washing in specific areas would make certain the cleansing was thorough at the end.

Linda made her introduction to Bill. We joined in a short conversation with the two of them, then left the room for privacy's sake. After her visit, Linda would go over her care plan with all of us so that either of the aides could provide his personal care. I would inform MK and Anna of our discussion at the office. We would also determine the overall schedule in the house after Linda's assignment of the number of hours and visits she would order for his care.

While Linda was doing her job, the four of us gathered for a brief time on the porch outside for some gulps of fresh air and water that we brought with us along with the cleaning supplies. The kitchen had to be tackled yet before we would take any food and beverage inside to enjoy. That and the upstairs bathroom were next on the agenda for the week. As we refreshed our bodies and rid the odor from inside, we talked together about our thoughts in general and specifically about Bill's care, as well as his brothers'. We were just realizing that we had not seen Arnie or Caleb this whole time. What a strange relationship existed among these siblings. Patty and I shared the day we sat around the kitchen table with Helen and all three of them while they remembered times of their youth on the farm. They seemed very connected then. We wondered aloud - did our little team have questions or personal misgivings about the situation at hand? We laughed as we made silly suggestions as to what the boys might be hiding. Gold? Stolen jewelry? Women? It was good to laugh. It provided short-term relief for our concerns. We all wanted to make things right. Patty and I wanted to fix it for Helen.

The care plan was rather normal and included cleanliness, out-of-bed activity, diet planning, medication management, and assistance with ADLs (activities of daily living) as needed. The order was two hours, three days for two weeks. It was easy to discuss, fitting it in with the housekeeping project. At a point in time, one of the swat team could concentrate on Bill's care while the other two continued the cleaning. They were a mighty crew!

After the schedule was settled, I left to return to the office while Patty, Jane and Ginny stayed to finish the day and plan for the next.

At that point, I guessed that I was the leader, per se. So, I walked up to talk with Bill about his care and how we would schedule it.

"I trust you, Patty," he said to me. "I feel better having you here." He unknowingly increased my confidence about completing this mission thoroughly!

After I talked with Bill, clean clothes were located. Jane helped him with a sponge bath from a basin. He dressed himself, walked to a chair that was in his room and sat down comfortably.

"Feel better?" I asked him as I returned from thoroughly checking out the bathroom. He replied with a smile. "Is there something to eat?"

Ginny had located Arnie and Caleb while we were doing these other things. They walked into the room just then. "Arnie and Caleb are happy to help us get this house cleaned up and will see that Bill gets food and is helped in the bathroom. We have an agreement, don't we, gentlemen?" Ginny asked with a smile.

Arnie answered for the two brothers, "Yes, ma'am."

Ginny added, "There is some canned soup in the kitchen and some crackers that seem fresh enough for their dinner this evening. We talked about their likes and dislikes and about their culinary skills." She took a break in her announcement for a little laugh and winked at the two. "I will go to the store this evening and pick up a few things to get them going for a few days and give them the receipt in the morning. We can pick it up from there after we have finished the cleaning. Everyone OK with this plan?"

Another smile from her and a wink to the two boys. "Absolutely," the five of us agreed at once.

When I arrived home that evening, I was singing. I still had an overpowering odor in my head, but I was happy. Go figure! Chet welcomed me from the kitchen while he was preparing dinner. I called to him from the door that I was going up to shower, wash my hair, and put on some clean clothes before I gave him a hug and had dinner. I was hopeful that I would smell good when I came back down the stairs. I always wanted to look good for Chet – not my best at times, but always because I cared about our marriage.

When I emerged in the kitchen, I was clean, my hair was clean, dried, and wound in a clip at the back of my head, and I was wearing an outfit that I knew he liked. Very casual, not fancy. I think it was the colors that he admired. I looked pretty good, and I did not smell! Dinner was delicious and we shared our day with each other over a cup of coffee and dessert. I had a great night's sleep knowing that the three of us had made some headway.

While MJ was still with us on day one, we agreed that we would return to clean two or three days in a row. We could do the personal care duties according to that schedule. So, the following day – day two of the cleaning team – we all met in the parking area at 8:00 a.m. Day two meant the upstairs bathroom and some of the kitchen if there was time. We decided before we went in that morning that two of us would tackle the bathroom and one the kitchen so that the boys could at least eat food on a clean plate off a clean table. Bill should be able to make it up and down the stairs for a meal with his brothers. We agreed we would "test" that idea before suggesting it.

Ginny chose the kitchen first and Jane and I reluctantly accepted the upstairs bathroom. There was no choice – but we giggled together as we discussed appointing Ginny to do the downstairs bathroom while we assigned ourselves to something not so ghastly as our upcoming task!

After sticking our heads into Bill's bedroom to say hello and walking down the hall to locate Arnie and Caleb to greet them with a good morning, Jane and I stood in the doorway of the bathroom to survey the scope and difficulty of our job. Actually, it seemed to us that the facilities themselves were in decent shape. Filth and disorder were our rivals.

Jane went into Bill's room to retrieve the supplies we had hastily left yesterday. I heard her speaking to Bill. He sounded well and said that when someone could help him, he'd like to get cleaned up and into his chair. I think I might have choked when I heard that. Then I smiled…"did that little bit of work make such a difference in him?" I prayed that the answer was "Yes" and decided to start with the toilet so that was off of my list of to-dos.

When Jane returned with the supplies, she asked, "Did you hear what Bill said to me?" I answered in the affirmative. We quietly looked at each other with knowing looks and got to work. She decided to tackle the tub/shower.

I was so thankful that Ginny had gotten the toilet unclogged the previous day. Cleaning it now with Lysol and a brush was not as bad as I thought it would be. Of course, there was much to scrub out, but with the water and the chemicals, it was not difficult. I flushed once. Cleaned and sanitized once more and flushed again. The toilet was working well! I cleaned the seat and tank top with the Lysol and sighed with satisfaction.

I looked over at Jane and she was having more trouble than I trying to clean the dirty ring from the inside of the tub. She was persistent and tried a few different cleaning solutions before the dirt began to disappear. Slowly, the whole tub was beginning to look white again. As with the toilet, the plumbing, faucets, and shower head were in working order. Thank goodness.

As she finished the tub, I cleaned the sink. I pulled out the stopper and removed hair twisted around it after I noticed that the water that I had run into the basin was barely draining. The cleanser cleaned up the porcelain and, so, voila, there was a white sink!

While the entire job to this point was not as difficult and disgusting as we anticipated, it had still taken us a good deal of time. When we were finished with the facilities, I volunteered to wash the floor on my hands and knees if Jane would empty the bucket of dirty water when needed, and return to me with new, clean water. Otherwise, she located clean towels and took the dirty ones to the washer while I was finishing up the floor.

Jane had to help me up from my knees after I wrung the cloth I was using for the last time and moved the bucket into the hallway. It had been emptied and refreshed three times. We both surveyed our fabulous work in silence. After the floor was dry, I would remove the shower curtain and throw that in the washer with the towels tomorrow, determined as I was that it would look like a hotel bathroom when completed! The two of us shared a high five, hugged and giggled. We didn't realize it right away, but all three of the boys had watched our little celebration. When we turned around and saw them standing there – even Bill in his

PJs – they actually looked different to us. Who would have guessed?

The five of us walked down the stairs together. Bill hesitated at first but navigated the trip well with the protection of his brothers; one went ahead, and one walked behind. When we walked into the kitchen, we saw the sun shining brightly through the window. As it landed on an appliance or other surface, the light did not fade from darkness or dirt. It was glowing in cleanliness! We all felt giddy.

Ginny had brewed a pot of coffee and the six of us sat down to a cup. What a feeling. "Good work, guys," I said to everyone. There was still quite a lot to do, but the most challenging tasks, except the downstairs bathroom, had been accomplished. After his cup of coffee, Bill walked slowly back up the stairs with Ginny to wash up and get dressed for the day. Jane and I stayed with Arnie and Caleb who were both quite good company. Who would have guessed?

Tomorrow would be another day. I actually looked forward to it.

We met at 9:00 a.m. the next day. Jane had to take her father to the senior center again. He fought the thought of spending time with the old people at first, but recently had adjusted to it and told others that he kind of liked it. Of course, he complained to Jane about everything while she was driving him home.

The boys were in the kitchen having coffee and toast when we walked in. The kitchen was still clean and in order. Bill was still in his PJs waiting for one of us to help him with his morning routine. They were talking about their mother. They missed her and were reminiscing a bit.

"Well, gentlemen, you seem cheery this morning!" Jane excitedly piped. "Is the toast all you are having for breakfast? Do we need to make a good grocery list and purchase other things for you to eat? What do you like that you don't have for breakfast or lunch?"

"Cereal, sausage, eggs, sandwich meat, soda" …the list went on with all three adding to the discussion at the same time.

"Here's our chance," I thought. I smiled internally. I knew that if anyone saw me winking at Jane, it would give me away. "Since

Jane and I cleaned the upstairs bathroom yesterday, why don't you do the downstairs one today, Ginny? It is smaller and I believe a little less dirty. Jane can get the washer going with the towels and shower curtain and help Bill with his cleanup and dressing. Perhaps a shave, Bill? I will work with Arnie and Caleb on the grocery list and then go to the store. Does that work with everyone?" Jane, of course, was pleased.

Ginny answered with a quiet, "OK." The boys looked at each other and nodded their heads.

We all began our assigned jobs.

Before I left, the boys gave me cash for the groceries. There did not seem to be a problem with the amount. They handed me much more that I believed was needed. However, thinking of Helen, I quickly realized that they had probably never done the grocery shopping.

To make a long story short, day three finished with a clean kitchen and bathroom downstairs and a clean bathroom (looking like a hotel) and bedroom upstairs. Groceries were in the cupboard and refrigerator and clean towels and clothing were ready for use. Bill was clean and walking with confidence and appropriate caution. The three boys were talking together and socializing with their swat team members. Bill had been served two hours of aide services three times that week. There was still work to be done – basic dusting and vacuuming of the other rooms, routine changing of linens, and maintenance of the cleanliness. The boys had to be involved with planning and scheduling as they went along, but for now, our little swat team went home for the weekend. On Tuesday, we would see the Short family again and find out how they fared on their own.

Tuesday's weather was perfect. Clear, blue skies, and a comfortable temperature for that time of year. My weekend had been terrific and my aide work on Monday was productive. My clients at the time were pleasant and not demanding. I enjoyed helping them according to their care plan and general needs.

Like clockwork, Jane, Ginny, and I all arrived within minutes of each other that morning. Again, it was a 9:00 a.m. start so Jane could take her father to the center. When we arrived at the door, the three boys welcomed us in. "Good morning," they choroused. They were smiling, well-dressed and groomed. Bill had apparently shaved again. They were no longer boys, but gentlemen. What a startling transformation!

We all went into the kitchen together. It was still rather clean. The brothers told us of their weekend, what they ate and what they did. It sounded like a good weekend to me except the food was a little boring – eggs and cereal. Caleb said, "We still need you; you know. We don't know how to keep track of what we need to do. We need a schedule with assignments on it for us to follow. We need instructions. We have never done the laundry, cooked (we were lucky this weekend), gone to the grocery store, made our beds... Mom did everything for us. We never learned these things. We rarely went anywhere beyond the farm and these days, there is no farming to do. That's where our life was and where we knew how to do things. We never had outside jobs. We have a man who manages our money and pays our bills. Mom set all of that up for us. Is it possible that you stay with us another week or so to help us?" I was stunned that they not only realized these realities, but they were also able to organize the thought and offer such a verbal acknowledgement.

And so, it was. That day we had Caleb, Arnie, or Bill shadow us as we dusted, vacuumed, and cleaned up the other two bedrooms upstairs. Those rooms weren't too bad. General cleaning and organization needed. They all needed to learn to put clothes away when they were clean and put them into a hamper or laundry basket when they weren't. The floor was a no-no, we laughingly told them.

Bill received his personal care while Caleb and Arnie sat with Jane and I at the kitchen table, paper, and pencil in hand, to begin listing and scheduling chores on a day per day, week per week basis. Each was assigned and the assignments were rotated. Other, less frequent chores were listed on a separate page. We agreed on a

list of instructions and training that were necessary – all participating in each. It was an interesting task and hopefully one they
could maintain. These gentlemen were intelligent. Their lives had
been handled with care by someone else and they apparently never
thought there could be any other way. I was sad for them. Helen
was amazing and loving. I was shocked, however, by the way her
love overshadowed much of their lives and impeded their
emotional growth and their opportunity to become unique individuals. She was the center of their universe for more than fifty years.
Hard to understand and rather heartbreaking. How curious it was
to be around them while Helen was alive and then to get to know
them when she wasn't. Magically they actually "wore" their own
personalities. Each was handsome in his own way. All three had a
terrific sense of humor.

The training days were over. Bill, Caleb, and Arnie each could
do the laundry, wash, and dry the dishes, clean the bathrooms,
make their beds, clean the several types of flooring, cook according
to simple recipes, and go to the grocery store. Surprisingly, Bill and
Arnie had driver's licenses. As we suggested, they phoned their
financial advisor who worked with them on making a budget. And,
as all of this was taking place, our little team continued to take care
of cleaning details like washing curtains, cleaning light fixture
covers of dead bugs, cleaning baseboards and trivial things that
most people never see. Bill's Medicare order expired, and he was
doing very well.

After a difficult start, the six of us learned how to be the best of
team players. We became very fond of each other. Jane, Ginny, MJ,
and I all visited the boys...wait, men... periodically to check up and
catch up. Over time, they individually stepped out into new public
lives they found through attending church, participating in
committees, and the frequent socials that were held. They once
boasted that they each made a dish for a potluck supper!

Together, we generated a happy ending.

Sandy

HAVING TO HOLD ON

I HAD BEEN SEEING Margaret three days a week for about three months. She was a nice lady who, if unable to stay at home with adequate assistance, would have been placed in a nursing home. She could not manage her personal care without assistance but helping her was not difficult. Margaret had a good, sharp mind and a fun, witty personality. I was glad that she did have the help she needed and could stay, at least for now, in her home. Margaret was ninety years old and somewhat frail. She had a bedside commode to use when she was alone so that she did not invite a fall when using the bathroom. She could use her walker. However, unsure of her balance, she only used it to get up and pivot to the commode when she was alone or for short walks when she was attended. She retained her continence, both of bowel and bladder.

There were other aides who came in when I was not scheduled. She also had a social worker who kept tabs on her, and kind neighbors who came to visit and bring a prepared meal to her once or twice a week. A lady from her church drove her to necessary appointments. Aside from her personal care, we collectively cleaned, did the laundry, and shopped for her. She was just one of many clients that the Agency served who were all alone. Even with her aides and the neighbors, she was alone for long hours, especially those she slept. She had an alert emergency button around her neck that she could use, if necessary, but I still hated the thought of her being alone through the night.

My schedule was to see her at noon that day. It wasn't the best time to see her because she would be eating her lunch but, of course, there would be time for her personal care later and while she was eating, I could do laundry, clean and/or prepare something for her dinner if nothing had been provided by someone else.

"Hi, Sandy!" she hollered from her room when she heard me walk in and close the door. I became concerned when I heard that voice. It was very unusual for her to be in her room at that time of day!

"Margaret, why are you in your room at lunchtime?" I asked as I walked down the hall.

When I entered her room, she flashed her usual smile and welcomed me cheerfully. She seemed to be in a great mood. "Didn't anyone come to help you this morning?"

"Yes, they came. But I felt tired, so while they were still here, I came back to bed. I have a little headache but mostly, I'm only tired." she said as she was giving me her update.

"I hope you are not getting a cold or the flu or anything. It is that time of year, you know. But I would hope that an aide or neighbor would not come in if they were sick."

"I don't know," she remarked. She then giggled, "Just want to be lazy, I guess."

"Well, you rest for a little more while I clean up a bit; maybe clean up the bathroom. Do I need to do any laundry?"

We worked it out that I would run some laundry and clean the bathroom. There was only one load, and the bathroom wasn't bad, so I knew I could bathe and dress her in some clean clothes and maybe do some other chores within the two hours that I was scheduled to be there. After that, I was going to see another client in the area – someone newly assigned. It was a two-hour job and then I would be going home.

My husband, Dan, who was a bit older than me, would have gotten home earlier and be able to prepare dinner for the two of us and our special needs son, Riley. Riley was delayed in intellect and clear speech and had been born with two holes in his heart. Blessedly, the holes closed up by the time he was walking, and his beating heart had kept him relatively healthy. But who would know what the future would hold with his difficult start? At twenty years old, he was pretty much tied to my apron strings and was safe, but very anxious about being home alone during the day. I loved him and was happy to care for him, but sometimes it became aggravating, and I minded the interruptions. When I substituted for the scheduler in the office every now and then, he would often call me. He would tell me he was having lunch. He would ask where to find something in the house. He always found what he thought were acceptable excuses to call and hear my voice. Luckily, the office team tolerated his frequent calls. Dan was good with him and when we were all at home – or together elsewhere – times were enjoyable. We were a solid family and respected Riley and each other. Sometimes it was tough, but that's the way it was.

While Margaret ate her lunch that had been delivered just after I arrived (my friend from church was the Meals on Wheels volunteer that day, which was a fun surprise), I cleaned the toilet, sink and tub in her bathroom. The tub was just a rinse out. She hadn't used that for a while. Safety always came first. For an aide, that was common sense. Her basin or sink baths had become routine and met her needs very well. The bathroom floor wasn't bad, so I thought I would clean it on my next visit. The washer had just stopped, so I put the things in the dryer and started it.

"Sandy let's use the commode here by the bed today. Is that OK with you? Maybe you can wash me up when I am sitting on it after I go," Margaret called out to me.

"Sure, that's fine," I answered. So, we worked together to get her onto the toilet.

I finished putting the cleaning supplies back where they belonged and then peeked in the bedroom to check on her. She looked a little pale but looked comfortable seated on the commode. "Are you OK"? I asked.

"Yes" was her response. Just a bit later, she called to say she was ready for her bath.

We chatted about something while I undressed her and got her ready. I have no idea what we talked about. I had the basin of very warm water ready – she liked it as hot as tolerable. We both heard the buzz of the dryer at that point. "Why don't you get the stuff out now. Then it's done and things won't be so wrinkled from laying in there," she said.

I looked at her rather incredulously. Here she was naked on the commode, the water ready for use and she wanted me to take care of the clothes! "Go ahead. Won't take you long. Just throw a towel over me. I'm fine."

She looked right at me while she said this, and she did sound fine. "Ok," I said.

I placed a towel over her, covering the parts that were most importantly protected and went to the dryer to take the clothing out. Most of it was dry, but there were a few pieces that seemed a bit damp yet.

"Margaret," I called out, "I am going to quickly fold the stuff that is dry. I had to put a few pieces in again which should be good by the time I do the folding. I'll take them out then. Just a few minutes more." She didn't acknowledge me, but I barely thought about it. I was busy with the laundry and my own thoughts, I guess.

The folding went fast. Underwear, night clothes, pants, and shirts. Only a few pieces that would have wrinkled, but they were done, now. I took the other things from the dryer. They were dry enough. I just laid them neatly on top of the folded clothes so I could get back to Margaret. "I'm coming, I'm coming," I sang out in a musical silly way to make her laugh.

As I walked into her bedroom, I intuitively knew that something was wrong. She was not sitting in her usual straight position, but she was slumping and looked uncomfortable. The towel had slipped a bit. Then I noticed her face. My God. My God! I know I was screaming! I was scared to approach her but got myself together quickly and ran over to her. I put my hand over her nose and watched her chest for movement. No breath. No breathing movement. Her pale, crooked face and fixed eyes told me that she truly had left us. Left me! She was, in fact, dead. "What to do? What to do?" I thought as I stared at her, hoping I was wrong and that she had just fallen asleep. "No, Sandy. She is not asleep," I said to myself hoping to be wrong. What happened? God, God help her! Help me!

"Margaret, Margaret, wake up!" I begged her.

I gave her arm a tiny shake and it slowly slid off of the arm of the toilet frame. No life. I started crying and bending over in shock. I wanted to vomit. Was the room spinning?

"God, please help," I prayed out loud and looked up toward the ceiling hoping for assurance that He was truly listening.

"Sandy, Sandy, think. Calm down. Think," I coached myself.

I went to Margaret's phone and dialed 911. I have no idea what I said during that call, but someone told me they would come. That's all I remember.

I then dialed the Agency office. The scheduler answered. "I need to talk to MK or Anna right away. It's Sandy, I said.

Liddy must have heard the fear and urgency in my voice. "They're not here, I'll get Lizzie," was the response.

Lizzie picked up the phone almost immediately. "Hey, Sandy, what's up?"

"Lizzie, I am at Margaret Sills house. She's dead on the commode!" I thought I had spoken clearly although my hands were shaking, and I was crying. Lizzie heard me!

"Oh my God, Sandy. Did you call 911?"

"Yes, and they are sending someone. But can you please come? I need someone."

"I'll come right over. Won't take me long," said Lizzie. She hung up.

Margaret lived in a town near the Agency office. I later learned that Lizzie, thankfully, knew where the house was because she had to deliver lunch to Margaret a few days before because of an emergency with a volunteer. That was a good thing because the house was off the street, tucked in a small void that separated two other homes situated mostly in front of it. They were larger and sat along the Main Street sidewalk. It was hard to even see Margaret's home unless you were really looking for it.

As I waited for the police and Lizzie, I sat with Margaret and tried to focus my mind on the lovely person she was with such a cheerful outlook about her situation. We enjoyed laughing together. I thought of the old, flowered housedress which was her favorite. With every washing cycle, the bright cheerful colors became dimmer and the fabric a bit thinner. But she loved it. She had a shawl that she often wore – black and beautifully made by a friend of hers.

I reflected on the life she had lived that she said was a "good one." She never told me many stories that would relate to any hurt or suffering she experienced. She told me warm stories of love and meaningful, happy days. Still, the emotions of one who was sitting with a lifeless body flooded over me. I was cold and shaky as I continued sending my prayers up to God for both of us. I was stuck in the reality of the moment and focused once or twice on my own breathing, just to make sure. I remember tears running down my face, but I also knew I had to compose myself. I got up and found a warm, soft blanket and draped her with it so that her body would not be exposed to the people who would arrive. And I didn't want her to be cold.

I talked myself into closing her eyelids. I recalled movies or TV shows when someone did that after a death. I stood straight and tall and talked encouragingly to myself and I tried to recreate the process. It worked and her eyelids were closed. I cried some more and looked at Margaret as I stepped back to distance myself. She looked very peaceful. I knew that she had been lovingly taken from this earth.

When I heard the knock on the door, such a strong feeling of relief went through my whole body. I could never adequately describe it to anyone. I hurried to open it to two uniformed police officers.

"The ambulance is on its way," one of them said to me. I was sure my legs were going to let me down at that point, but I was able to get myself together and continued standing. I said some things to them that I don't remember, and then led them into her bedroom where poor Margaret still sat on the commode covered neck to toes with the blanket. I noticed shocked looks on their faces when they saw her sitting there. Both faces then turned into a combination of pity and grief. "Neither was past his thirties and although this wasn't new to them," I thought, "it wasn't anything they experienced often, even considering deaths in their own families." It was about that time that I noticed that both the blanket and Margaret had slipped down a bit. I knew that her weakened and limp muscles must be the cause of this sliding and not rigor mortis, but either way, she had to be pulled back up or moved from the commode to the bed. I thought to myself that I would protect her privacy and move the blanket along with her as the police officers got her into her bed.

"Can you please help here, officers? Margaret needs to be moved into her bed." I said. "I will keep her covered while you move her. She is sliding from the commode a little." I certainly thought that this was not an extraordinary thing I was asking of them, but their response froze me.

One of them answered, "Ma'am, we are not permitted to move or touch a body until the coroner has pronounced them deceased."

"What???" I think perhaps the neighbors might have heard me! "Why? We can't just leave her like this! When is the coroner coming? Has he been called?"

"Yes, Ma'am," was the reply. Just then, I heard someone knocking at the door. I assumed it was the EMTs and the ambulance or better yet, the coroner, and ran to the door. It was Lizzie!

"Thank God you are here," I said as I hugged her. By this time, I was a little out of my mind again and was not altogether sure what

I was saying or how I looked and sounded. I wanted to calm down but just couldn't.

"The ambulance is right behind me," Lizzie said, as I released her from my hug. I saw she had the start of tears in her eyes, but maybe it was for me??? She maintained a calm exterior. While I waited for the ambulance to park and EMTs to come to the door, Lizzie went to talk to the police who were still standing in the same spot they assumed when they originally entered the room. Apparently, Lizzie learned about the regulations they had to obey regarding touching and/or moving the body.

Three EMTs, two men and one woman, came to the door rolling a gurney along with them. As I let them in and pointed to Margaret's room, I thought this would be over soon. I let out a sigh of relief and sorrow for it would become reality that I would no longer see or laugh with Margaret.

"Where is Dr. Martin?" one of them asked as he turned from viewing Margaret to speak to me. One of the police answered that they did not know.

Lizzie spoke up. "Do you guys also have to abide by the do-not-move regulation, too?"

"Yep," was the reply.

I looked at Margaret who had moved down a slight bit more. "This is crazy! Can't you see that she needs to be moved to her bed before she eventually slides to the floor? I assume Dr. Martin is the coroner. Where IS he?" I was very agitated and had no understanding of this ridiculous protocol, especially with the EMTs who took vitals, etc. every time they responded to a call.

"We were told that he is on the golf course. They paged him, though."

The police officer who offered the information was a bit reticent to tell us as he did not look at us when he spoke. I wanted to curse at him, but of course, I did not. It certainly would not have helped the situation. And I don't curse. I found myself praying to God to get that coroner off of the golf course.

"Doesn't this man have a job to do?" I heard Lizzie's raised voice ask. "What is he doing playing golf at this time on a week-day?" Now, I clearly knew how Lizzie felt. She was not just angry, she was livid.

There was a lot of silence and quiet discussion between the professionals for a long time. They were unable to help poor Margaret. Lizzie and I, with good reason, stood on either side of Margaret and the commode to make certain that she did not slide onto the floor. If Lizzie thought there was a liability with us touching her, she said nothing about it. Of course, we were not going to move her to the bed, because at this time, she would be more difficult to move. We stood there with her, our hands lightly gripping her upper arms to make sure she would no longer slide. We looked into each other's eyes often and tried, through our own gaze, to reassure the other. We spoke to each other quietly that she was in Heaven experiencing a beautiful peace.

An hour had elapsed since I dialed 911 when the coroner, Dr. Martin showed up in his golfing attire. He pronounced Margaret deceased, and I held the blanket in front of her as the EMTs moved her onto the gurney and placed her in the ambulance. It was a difficult yet welcome sight to see them drive away.

Meanwhile, Lizzie calmly spoke to Dr. Martin and thanked him for his service. The police officer told me that they had my "statement," and I could leave.

Lizzie helped me clean the commode, make the bed, and empty the basin of water. I carefully folded the dry clothes that I hadn't gotten to and moved all of them to her room. I don't believe we left any evidence of the "event" for next of kin to see when we closed the door behind us. Lizzie went back to work, and I went home. Thankfully, the office had already sent another aide to my next client.

It started to rain as I drove to the house. It was apropos.

Lizzie wrote a letter to the County and State health officials about the situation, Dr. Martin, and the ridiculous regulations. A few years later, the law was passed that nurses and other medically trained professionals were allowed to pronounce death.

Lizzie

THEFTS, GUNS, AND DRUGS

"THIS IS a hell of a lot worse than just the theft itself," I thought. On my second or third day with the company, I received a call from a client accusing the aide of stealing from her. When I asked what was stolen, she replied that it was a very valuable object! I remember being horrified – I was here to make certain that the Agency and its personnel did an excellent job, and the clients were cared for properly. I was so upset and nervous. I was around when employees stole from my father's business, so I wasn't unfamiliar with the fact that there are bad eggs in every group or organization. The stolen article was not the only matter, however. The Aide, the Agency...yikes! Litigation, the newspaper! My mind was racing as I, of course, drove to the client's house to assume my responsibilities.

Rebecca greeted me at my car after I parked in the driveway. She was a younger aide who had recently completed her training. "I didn't take anything, Lizzie. I didn't steal a silver tablespoon."

Her tears were streaming down her face, and I instantly believed her. I was so emotionally involved with that poor girl that it didn't hit me right away. Then my mind went back into gear. "A silver tablespoon is what this is all about?" I queried.

"Yes," Rebecca responded. "Mrs. Warner insists that I have taken it. She has three drawers full of silverware – all laying loosely about. If this were truly a valuable item, wouldn't it be somewhere else... in a box or something?" Her line of thought worked for me.

"Let's go in to talk with her", I said as I started walking to the house. "I have to find that spoon," I thought. I admit that I was very annoyed but felt so sorry for Mrs. Warner who obviously believed something she loved and wanted was missing. As soon as I walked through the kitchen door, she began verbally attacking me as the leader of thieves who were taking advantage of old people!

I quietly walked up to her and held out my hand to shake hers as I introduced myself as the Executive Director of the Agency – Rebecca's boss. With a questioning and strained face, Mrs. Warner shook my hand. I sighed an inward sigh knowing I had somehow quieted her anxiety a bit.

"I understand that a silver tablespoon is missing," I said calmly. "The three of us can search for it. What does it look like?" I asked.

Unfortunately, Mrs. Warner could not give us a clear picture of the item. She stammered and stammered saying "It's a spoon. A silver spoon. A spoon."

We each took a drawer as I suggested and began looking for a silver tablespoon. Actually, there were several, but I found one that was obviously designed much differently from the other silverware I was encountering. So, I took a chance. "Is this the one you are looking for?" I asked.

Mrs. Warner's face lit up. Smiling at us, she said "Yes. That's it! Thank you. Thank you."

Rebecca turned to me and whispered, "Thank you." I smiled at her and told her I hoped she would have a good day. Mrs. Warner was already fussing in the kitchen as if she were going to cook something with that spoon. As I walked to the car, I made a mental note to have a social worker visit. I wondered if the lady should be living alone.

This may have been the first, but there were other thefts for which an aide was accused. Unfortunately, there were those that were legitimate.

Another such event came to my attention through Anna. One day when she was making a visit to a client, she was met at the door by that client who was loudly accusing the aide of stealing all of her money. She had, just minutes before, called the police and they were on the way. Of course, Anna took the aide aside and spoke to her. The aide denied having taken anything. She had already asked the client to look through her purse and in her room, but no cash had been found. Anna told me the poor aide was a wreck and she thought she would be handcuffed and taken to jail. The police did arrive and after a sidebar with Anna, they spent time talking with the client. The aide sat still and waited for word from the police. Anna then told me that it had occurred to her that often the elderly hid things in the freezer. She looked in the refrigerator's freezer and found nothing. She then asked the aide if there was another freezer. There was one in the garage where a bag of cash was found, wrapped tightly and secured with rope. Happily, the story ended there.

One day while I was working at my desk, MK came to my door with an aide, Connie, who had some serious concerns about her client, Mrs. Richardson. I knew of Mrs. Richardson because she had been an important person in one of the notable towns in the county. She had served on the town council and was celebrated as a generous donor to organizations that provided for those in need in the community. She was a widow and lived in a beautiful home – commonly known as the Richardson estate. I had never met her, but I knew we had aides working there. She was a private client and one that never hesitated to ask for more time when she felt that she needed it. The aides enjoyed working for her. I happened upon a conversation among three of the aides who were working or had worked for her. They all loved her and told stories to each other about her uplifted spirit and the laughs they had with her. Apparently, she was a fun and gracious person who behaved as if she was unaware of her public standing. I noticed that none of them called her by her first name – it was always Mrs. Richardson. That in itself said a lot about their respect and care for her!

I had papers piled on one of the two chairs in my office, so I cleaned it off and both sat down to talk with me. Connie informed me that she thought that Mrs. Richardson's friends – a policeman and his wife that lived nearby – were stealing from her. She allowed them to handle her financial affairs including paying her bills and providing her money for other needs. Connie was only indirectly involved but enough to believe that money was disappearing into their hands. For instance, Connie did the grocery shopping using an account Mrs. Richardson had with the store. The store delivered the items and the receipt of the purchase. The officer or his wife would then settle the account with the store. Connie, feeling suspicious for no reason other than her instincts at the time, had the opportunity to look at Mrs. Richardson's checkbook. "I recorded checks that were written to the officer for payment of grocery bills," Connie stated. She related to me that she found that odd – why was the check not written to the grocery store?

After that realization, Connie recorded the amount of the weekly grocery receipt in a tablet she kept in her purse before she passed the receipt to the officer. He would then pay the store. "Lizzie, the amounts never matched. I even considered the dates of the checks thinking perhaps they were for more than one receipt or any other likely reason why it never balanced. It was obvious, then, to me that they were stealing from her account. And it was a weekly sum of at least fifty dollars. Mrs. Richardson had no way of knowing. She trusted them."

I became a bit annoyed, which turned into active anger, as Connie informed me that Mrs. Richardson complained about misplacing items in her home. Small antique items here and there. It befuddled her because she assumed she had moved them and forgotten where she placed them. Once or twice, it was a piece of her jewelry that had been handed down through her family. "She can't even find the earrings that mean a lot to her - the earrings she wore on her wedding day," Connie remarked with emotion.

"More than once I helped her look for the items she said were missing. And then it occurred to me that they were not misplaced at all. They had been stolen!" Connie asserted with conviction.

"What can we do, Lizzie? We can't just let this go!" she pleaded.

I was, of course, going to do something about the situation and told Connie and MK that I certainly would look into what could be done to eventually bring this to the legal system. "Thank you, Lizzie," Connie uttered as she rose and walked toward the door. "Please keep me informed. Meanwhile, I will behave as if I do not suspect anything. Of course, I will not tell Mrs. Richardson about any of this. Will you tell the other aides who have been in there that you are aware?" I nodded my head, yes.

I then called the attorney that sat on our Board. It was an uncomfortable situation to go to the police to report our suspicions about an officer who obviously served at the same station. As I spoke with our attorney, it became clear that I, as the representative of the organization, would make the report. The policy that I made before this situation was that our staff would never be involved at this level, and I never allowed them to be a witness or defend anyone in court. Those things would be my job if the courts accepted that it was my role. They had in the past. It was a difficult road this time.

After I reported it, the officer and his wife were picked up, questioned, and a future court date scheduled. Obviously neither of the two returned to help Mrs. Richardson.

Before the legal session, I became aware that if Connie did not come forth in court, the charge would probably be dropped. Neither Connie nor I wanted this case to be dismissed so I permitted her to testify. She prepared herself with the help of the attorney and one of the other aides who had also worked there was able to attend along with me. That helped Connie to relax a bit and the judge got to see that she had support of a colleague who probably could testify to the same. Thankfully, the case was settled on that first day and the officer and his wife were both found guilty. I never learned anything about their sentence or what happened to his position with the police.

Mrs. Richardson became a client with the County's Human Services Department. They arranged for someone at the bank to manage her funds. The aides continued to enjoy caring for her.

Guns? The next, and new, concern for me. One day one of the nurses came to me to explain an uncommon situation in a Medicaid client's house. Guns. Lots of guns. Maybe twenty. Most were in an open gun cabinet. Small handguns were found on tabletops in the living room and bedroom. Obviously, we were working with a strange situation to say the least. How would we know that the gentleman was not just an avid collector but one of the crazies who would harm someone? "Would he shoot the aide or nurse because he didn't like what they said?" I pondered. My head was spinning. After some rational thought, I called the local police, explained the situation, and asked if they would have an officer meet me at the client's home. I wanted to tell the client that we could not place an aide in the home because the guns would make them uncomfortable. I certainly would not express any – even the slightest - possibility that he might use the guns irresponsibly.

Things went well. A policeman was with me as I spoke to the gentleman about my concerns.

"I have collected guns for years," he told us after we had introduced ourselves and I politely told him of my concern for our aides. "None of them are loaded. I don't even know if I have any ammunition in the house." He pointed to one of the guns in the cabinet. "See – this one is from the Civil War," he proudly told us. It was easy to see that he was being truthful and, knowing nothing about guns, I still could tell that they were truly collectibles. I quickly liked the man and felt certain that he would never hurt anyone, but I couldn't send an employee in there without validation of my thoughts and there was no way to accomplish that.

"I believe you," I told him. "But I still feel uncomfortable asking my staff to be in this environment. I hope you understand." He politely and graciously told me that he did, and he would be fine. I thanked the officer and went back to my office to speak with the referral agency to explain that we could not fill the order. I was sorrowful. But I felt that I made the appropriate decision.

We received a Medicaid order one day for an aide to provide the full menu of our services: Personal care, range of motion exercises, light cleaning and laundry, grocery shopping and some meal prep. Unlike Medicare orders, Medicaid purchased more time for multiple chores, and it lasted much longer, timewise. Some Medicaid clients never left the service until they passed away. Medicaid was a State service that was granted for financial reasons - the clients did not have the financial resources to provide the help for themselves. I was always appalled at the income statements of some and wondered how they survived. But for the Agency, Medicaid was a budgetary nightmare. Their reimbursement to us – and all other nonprofits - was far lower than our average hourly cost (not rate) to provide the service. They were always way overdue to pay us. Months overdue. That seriously affected our cash flow and made payroll a knuckle-biting experience sometimes.

This order was for a ninety-eight-year-old lady who was mostly bedbound, although we were told that with assistance she could sit in a chair and perhaps use a walker to get to a bedside commode. I was the one who pulled the order from the fax machine that morning and handed it to Anna. We wondered why she did not have assistance. Was this aged lady all alone? The address was in town among the rowhomes which dotted one block. An aide was scheduled, and Anna, per regulation, added the assessment and care plan time to her calendar for the same morning.

The situation in the home came to my attention late that afternoon when Anna stopped at the office to get some paperwork completed before going home.

"Lizzie, this home is a mess. Ms. Jackson lives on the second floor in a room by herself. There are three other rooms up there and one bathroom that would make anyone feel sick. Donna can clean that up for her. She has a walker, but not a bedside commode. They have to get her that. But 'they' is the problem. When the door was opened to me, the first thing I noticed was young men – maybe five of them – smoking marijuana. There were pill containers on the table where they sat. There were a number of dishes of food and bags of chips and pretzels, as well. They were obviously just hanging out. Of course, the smoke filled the air. I was afraid I'd get high just walking in." We shared a laugh. "The men were pretty sleazy looking, Lizzie, and stared at me as if I was unwelcomed company. I said hello to them and asked where Ms. Jackson was. One answered that his great-grandmother was upstairs in bed. I walked through the kitchen - a stove and frig were there - and climbed the stairs. Her room was at the top and just to the right. She was sitting in her bed. She had a tray on her lap with breakfast leftovers and an unfinished cup of tea. I was confused. Did those raunchy kids bring her breakfast and tea on a tray?"

I was taking all of this in as she spoke. I pictured the scene around the table in my mind. "How would the aides feel?" I had to remind myself – as I always said to the aides, "Remember, we are guests in their home."

"Did Donna show up? Was she there to go over the care plan with you before you left? What did she have to say about the downstairs party?" I asked.

"Yes." Anna replied. "She came as scheduled and everything went well. She and Ms. Jackson will get along fine. Ms. Jackson is a darling."

I questioned her about the care plan and the number of hours we would suggest to the County Human Services worker. (These State funds were funneled through the County Social Services.) It all seemed realistic and sufficient. If any of the young men were living in that house, we would not cook for them or do their laundry. If they used the upstairs bathroom, then they would ultimately benefit from our service to Ms. Jackson. We would have to keep an eye on the situation with the drugs. If we reported them, Ms. Jackson might be left with nobody. I didn't think that marijuana punishment was harsh. Nevertheless, in this case, I felt that we had to turn our heads unless we saw a lot of people coming and going as if they were selling out of that kitchen.

This was a complicated situation I discussed with the County worker whom I knew quite well. We could easily talk in private and could trust each other to follow our agreed upon decision: Continue service to Ms. Jackson and send in a social worker or nurse a bit more often than required. The aides would be informed of the situation before they accepted the job. In other words, we would be diligent in our "supervision" and honestly call a STOP when we knew we should.

The aides that were routinely scheduled – Monday through Friday, two hours per day – learned to know all of the young men by their first names. As it turned out, all of them had decent, honest jobs, some with different shifts, so on an off day they got together with some weed. (Their words, not mine!) The pill dispensers were Ms. Jackson's and, yes, they had served her breakfast on a tray with her meds that morning. I often think of the lesson I learned from these young people and the respect they had for family, especially a ninety-eight-year-old. As I remember, we served her for almost a year. She didn't make her hundredth birthday.

There are so many other "short" stories that tell of the goodness of the aides who worked for our organization. They were amazing, gentle, caring, and patient people.

Lizzie

VISITOR IN COSTUME

I MET MJ in the parking lot that morning after I pulled my car in right behind hers. "Hey, good morning!" we both greeted each other. She walked up beside me with a big smile on her face. "Nice day, huh?" I nodded in agreement as I unlocked the back door and we both walked in. It was sunny and warm. This afternoon it would be hot, and we wanted to start the fans early in the day to get a jump on temperature inside the office. We had a few floor fans to cool us off. No AC and no ceiling fans. We had a number of windows to open and a screen door on each of the two floors. On the bright side, we did have a full kitchen and bath on each floor which helped us appreciate the building. And, also, it was ours!

I arrived in my office on the second floor and less than five minutes later, I had to run down the stairs to go out to my car and retrieve paperwork that I had taken home with me the evening before and neglected to bring it back to my desk that morning. As I was walking past the scheduler's desk, I saw MK and Anna hovering around it and talking about something. I slowed my pace and overheard MK saying to Liddy, who was the scheduler, "I'm not surprised she wouldn't do that evening job. She gets to Barnes just before six in the morning!" I thought, "huh??? That is awfully early."

Liddy said, "No, she doesn't. She's not scheduled until eight o'clock!" MK and Anna looked at each other with a concerned look, then faced Liddy again. They spoke a whispered response to her question, "She goes early on her own time to milk the cows, and gather eggs," they said.

I walked into the cubicle and said, "What did I just hear? What? Who are you talking about?" They all looked at me as if they had seen a ghost.

I waited patiently until MK said, "Stella goes to Sadlow's early to milk the cows – two of them – and gather eggs. She doesn't put it on her time sheet. But old Mr. Sadlow is ninety-five and he will not buy food from the grocery store. He wants his own. His eighty-one-year-old daughter, Hanna, takes care of the animals and garden."

They were all still watching me as I took in this news. I turned around without saying a word and proceeded to go out to the car, all the while thinking about this crazy world and the beautiful people in it. Who was I to upset the old man who depended upon his own crops and livestock to provide all that he needed - and lived longer than I ever will. I just prayed nothing would go wrong. Stella was an incredible lady, and I was not going to interfere. I quickly prayed that Stella would not be injured working with the animals.

Later that morning, I took a phone call from the hospital VN because I frankly couldn't stand to hear it ring any longer. Everyone else was tied up. The nurse wanted to give me a referral over the phone. "No problem. Glad to help."

We talked a little bit, asking about the family, the weather, and her upcoming vacation. We finally got to the referral. She started by telling me that the lady was blind. "OK." Then she told me she was also deaf. "OK."

Then I heard her start, "And, she..."

I said jokingly, "Is her name Helen Keller?" I giggled a bit and then the answer came to me from the other end of the line.

"Yes. That's her name. How did you know?" True story. Through the years we ran into numerous names that we will not easily forget. And with the team that we had; you can probably guess what some of them might have been. Hint: Peter Long. That one was mild. Others brought screams and "Oh no's," before the laughter.

The afternoon was not unlike the morning. I took several calls that required either a decision or a biting of the tongue. The hospital Home Health Executive Director, Maddie, phoned me to discuss a situation that involved an aide and their VN. Of course, in their mind, the aide was at fault due to her insistence on doing things her way and not as the VN instructed. I was not surprised because I knew both parties; the VN behaved arrogantly, and the aide was very sure of herself and her work. Maddie and I discussed the situation and I learned of the client's needs and schedule. I agreed to substitute a different aide, pulling the current one. I then asked Anna to personally make the change instead of the scheduler and make an appointment to talk with the aide who was pulled. As a nonprofit home care agency, there was no money for an HR person although with over one hundred employees, one could have been useful. Between me, Anna, and MK we managed all types of those affairs including hiring, training, vacation tracking, etc. Judy managed the Workers' Compensation business. In a case like this, we behaved as the supervisor and the advisor. Of course, when the situation came from Anna or MK to my attention again, it became a bit more serious for the employee.

To recharge myself, I made the second trip to the upstairs bathroom that day. The first was for obvious reasons – the second to visit the kittens. There was once a stray cat in the area that greeted us frequently in the parking lot in the morning. Of course, with an office full of animal lovers, we began feeding her. One day, she showed up with her husband and a bulging belly. We continued taking care of both of them, feeding them on the landing of the second-floor outdoor steps. We took notice one day that neither of them came for food and it remained that way for a few days. Then, one morning both showed up again and her belly was no longer bulging. We surmised that she had given birth and some other critter had enjoyed them. In our grief, we cared for them all the more – naming them Willie and Helen after clients of ours. Helen shortly thereafter became pregnant again and we watched her carefully. At the appointed time, we noticed her walking onto our property from the wooded area behind us with a kitten in her mouth. She climbed a tree easily with her cargo, dropped it into a crook in the tree, climbed down and left to get the next one. She carried six newborn kittens into that crevice between two very thick limbs. We were amazed that she was probably saving these babies from what we assumed was a devastating outcome for her previous litter. As it happened, there was a severe weather warning issued for late that afternoon and we worried that the babies would drown from the heavy rain that was expected. MJ went home and returned with a ladder. She climbed up, reached into the tree and, one by one, handed the babies down to me. Helen did not mind. The babies grew up in the bathtub in the second-floor bathroom. Helen was a great mom. We kept the bathroom window open, and she came and went as she pleased. Willie was constantly by her side when she was outdoors. We found homes for all babies but one...Moses ended up living fourteen happy and comfortable years with me and my dog.

Back to the reality of the day...

Again, the phone was for me. I was hopeful it was one of my colleagues in the State Organization of Nonprofit Home Care Agencies or from the Commission on Accreditation for Home Care. I was on the standards committee of the new accreditation organization. We free-standing nonprofit home care agencies in the state began this endeavor to "police" ourselves - one in each county of the State. Word got to the State Department of Human Services who questioned if we would collaborate with them to introduce standards that would be followed by all organizations – profit or nonprofit - who wanted to bill Medicaid directly. If the standards were not upheld, Medicaid would no longer work with that organization. As it turned out, the agreement was signed and sealed, and our original nonprofit organization to which we all belonged acted in the management of both agencies. I thoroughly enjoyed our work to review, maintain, and/or update the standards of our business quality that those we served deserved.

But no. The call was from the Director of Human Services for the County. To me, he was an adversary, even though he did sign on the dotted line for a bit of County funding for the Agency. Doing business with this man was exceedingly difficult. To put it bluntly, he did not like strong, independent women. There were four of "us" in this county and he took turns targeting us. One after another, then another, and another and back to the original victim again. I was not just a strong woman, but a very honest one. That has always been my goal – to be remembered as an honest and fair administrator. But this gentleman wanted in the worst way to find something dishonest or even fraudulent going on in the organization. I was always careful to tell the office staff when I had to meet with him or talk to him. They knew to leave me alone for a while afterward because I was always upset or angry. Of course, this day, I took the phone call.

He questioned me about some line items in the financial report I had just forwarded to him in obeyance of the requirements for County funding. The man was completely ignorant of our business which didn't help our relationship or quality of our communication. Of course, he questioned expenditures and – unbelievably – why we used so many gloves? Can you imagine – all these aides and additional nutrition workers in three kitchens, packing up and serving food and he wondered why our glove expenses were so high? Was I using that money for other things that I could not submit on a budget, he inquired? I did a respectable job that day, as I remember. I ended the conversation in a professional manner. I then hung up the phone and then began ranting.

I heard my upstairs team who could hear bits and pieces of the conversation through my opened office door clapping and laughing to get me out of my dither – they were pretty successful but, I needed more. I closed my office door, dressed as the Unknown Executive Director, and proceeded to walk through the office, upstairs and down. This nutty performance was put together some time ago (motivated by the Unknown Comic on *Laugh-In*, a favorite TV show at the time). It helped me to downgrade my importance so I wouldn't get so emotional with the difficult parts of my position. I was downstairs doing my parade amidst giggles and "We know who you are and where you live!" comments, when I heard Ginny say, "Who is that?" followed by laughter that doubled her over. She had come into the office to pick up her paycheck. Of course, few people other than my staff knew that I could be such an idiot sometimes.

The person whose identity she was questioning had a sign hanging from a string around her neck that read, The Unknown Executive Director. The head – and identity of that person – was covered by a brown paper bag with two eyeholes cut out of it. I stood as still as I could, looking at Ginny, holding a statuesque posture. Shortly after, I took off the bag and noticed that some were still laughing a bit, but others, shaking their heads in disbelief that their boss would behave this way, had gone back to work. Overall, though, the Unknown saved all of us an unusually quiet and uneventful afternoon!

We had an in-service that evening which I always looked forward to. Generally, I worked late and went directly to the meeting which started at seven o'clock. However, that night I had dinner plans with another female Executive Director in the county. When we met after work, we always chose the same restaurant for dinner that was situated halfway between our offices. It was rather upscale but very comfortable and the people friendly. As usual, the meal was great that evening.

I mentioned my telephone encounter that afternoon and told her of his accusations toward my financial handling of county funds. She, also, had received a phone call from him that day. Their conversation, as well, angered her. The topic of that call was a complaint about her handling of a recent problem with an abused child. Her summation to me of her part of the conversation was, "The law is the law. I cannot change it despite what others may feel."

We each toasted the other with our glass of wine - hers white, mine red – and began the usual conversation of our personal lives.

After dinner, I drove to the in-service with an altered mood – doesn't wine, good food, and good company provide an unburdening? I arrived at the meeting somewhat later than usual, but being with the team of aides and staff that had already gathered when I arrived maintained my positive outlook. They always reminded me of the excellent work they were doing in our community and while our speaker held the floor that night, I quietly reflected on the many tales they could tell.

Stella

PITY THE LITTLE CHILDREN

I **LOVED** my job as a Home Health Aide for the Agency. I had some real adventures and warm experiences. I loved the work and the clients for the most part. Of course, there were those who were difficult people to please. Some required intervention by one of our nurses or Lizzie or from someone in administration at a referral organization.

I recall one such job several years ago. It was a Division of Youth and Family Services client, or DYFS as it was known. The case was a sad state of affairs and in retrospect, it was worse than that. It was pitiful. The job included several foster children in a home that was unfit, to put it politely. The situation with that family even made the local newspaper as intervention by DYFS was angrily reported to the press by the foster parents. I managed to continue working patiently with them, but to tell you the truth, I would have been glad to be relieved of it.

The reality of the conditions in the home was unconscionable. Two adult women who lived together were approved as foster parents at some point. After my experience with them, I was shocked to know that they had "passed the test" and I wonder even today how that happened. (Of course, I have my opinion on this, but that is for another time.) However, I must admit that they seemed to be caring – maybe even selfless individuals who really loved the children at first. I became aware that this was not the case rather quickly, however. As it turned out, the children were their paychecks while the State paid for me and other aides to take care of them. These ladies knew how to milk the system and had their own way for a long time. The situation was shameful. I was an unknowing and, later, a not so willing participant.

Let's be honest. My first impressions were of a house right on the road – practically no frontage - that needed painting and sported a brown grass and bare dirt front lawn. The house must have appeared abandoned to the drivers who passed by each day. Of course, after frequent passes, they probably no longer even noticed it. Driving to or from a busy day, you hope to see pleasant things.

There was a good bit of traffic that day. I frequently traveled that road through the small town. It was a heavily used route between the area's two main roads, each eventually arriving at thriving larger towns with stores, schools, and hospitals. The house showed no real signs of interest in life, pride, or joy as I viewed the front facade. Not even a flower or two - which made me question things even then. But, of course, I was very much a flower and color person, and others may not have even noticed what I did, much less judged the situation because of it. But it was dirt and brown grass! How could you not notice that anything attractive or with color was missing? I could taste the naked ground.

I was scanning the broken up and discarded toys on the front porch – a tricycle with flat tires, some GI Joe type dolls, a Candyland board, trashed coloring books and a broken-up play kitchen set - when I heard and saw three small children running from the back and around to the front yard, obviously near the busy road. No adults were with them. The kids were dirty and shabby. Holes or tears in their clothes here and there. Bare feet. They continued to run around even after they saw me standing there watching them. A little girl with long tangled blonde hair threw me a smile and giggled. My thoughts about these three unfortunately tracked along with my other first impressions of the home. But I was determined to have an open mind.

I understood that people led different lives from my own, which might include less cleanliness and no flowers in the yard. I scolded myself and talked myself into a better attitude. "The sky is blue, and the children looked happy, after all," I said to myself. I thought about the times when my brothers and I might have looked the same way as we played outside with sheer abandon! We were quite a little group. I am sure my mother probably thought she'd lose her mind sometimes. Our trio was loud, rambunctious and had no thoughts of others. Just us, having fun and creating mayhem. I laughed aloud thinking of one of our escapades – stealing Christmas cookies that Mom kept in tins, hidden in the shed. My mind and memory worked well together as I could see the look on Mom's face on Christmas Eve when she found one mostly empty tin among the others. So long ago, but so real to me when I let my mind remember when.

I parked the car behind the house in an area with a small swing set and more brown grass and dirt surrounding it. I knocked on the back door. I did not see the children and wondered where they had gone. Thoughts of that road raced through my mind. I shooed those thoughts away.

The two clients knew I was coming and even had a time of arrival for my visit, so I waited just a brief time for the knock to be answered as I watched ants busily taking food into their hole. I noted that their energy and focus were incredible. "Stella, I said to myself, you don't do so bad for an old lady," smiling at the thought. I had recently been concerned about letting my age slow me down. I really have trouble accepting that I am not even middle-aged anymore. The thought that I am old runs through my brain regularly and causes great mental turmoil!

I heard voices and looked up from the ants just as the door swung open to welcome me and there stood the two ladies. Smiling, pleasant, and appropriately dressed in nice clean clothes. "Please come in" one said.

I was a bit relieved to see the two of them obviously interested in my impression of them and their behavior. I walked in and we shook hands and made our introductions. The shorter one, and seemingly younger, introduced herself as Ann and the other, Katie. They were pleasant and showed me into a family room of sorts with TV, bookshelves with children's books placed on them, a few toys and comfortable seating. It was a bright room and quite clean. A window air conditioner cooled the room in the mid spring heat. The temperature was unusual for this time of year, but I still remembered the frosty winter and I was enjoying it just now. I knew I wouldn't later...I have always said, "You can put more on to stay warm but how much clothing can you possibly take off to stay cool?"

I was pleased with what I saw at that time, yet wondered if the children were ever allowed in that room. I silently chastised myself again. Six children can make the neat and clean into a mess in a hurry. Ann offered me coffee or iced tea. I declined because I was there to work and help with the children. DYFS had ordered the service from our Agency. I had been told there were six children, though.

"I saw three children playing out front when I drove in. I understand there are six children here. I assume three are in school?" I had noted their names and ages in my notes, which I unfortunately left in the car.

Katie answered, "Yes. There are three in school just now. Amy, Jack, and Melanie are in elementary school. Melanie is a special needs child, but that classroom is in the same building with the normal kids."

That word normal made me uncomfortable, for some reason. Understand, I am not one of those politically correct people, but it made me feel bad for the child that her "parents" saw her as abnormal rather than just a little behind the others. "You have not yet met Melanie," I thought to myself. "No judgements today."

"Who are the children playing outside and what are their names?" I asked. "I suppose these are the ones you have asked us for help with. I believe my hours are what you requested?"

"Those kids are Joey, Anthony, and Mary. Yes, for now," Katie said with an attitude of irritation and impatience. Her face showed the same. I didn't detect any warmth in her eyes.

She continued, "We have asked DYFS for help around dinner time, as well. The children need help doing their homework, the others may be cranky and tired, and the meal needs to be prepared. Ann and I are hoping we can all work together to have a smooth evening for the kids. And, of course, there is always cleaning and laundry to be done during the day."

She gave me a smug smile and looked at Ann. The overall demeanor of these two was proper, but I was skeptical of the emotion and reasons behind it. I was frankly a bit puzzled. I learned in the near future to trust my first impressions. I remember wondering to myself at that moment just what in the world did these two do with their time? Three little ones running around without supervision in dirt next to a road and three in school. "Stop it, Stella. You know better after all these years," I heard echoing in my head. I hate it when I catch myself doubting others' intentions when I don't even know them. (I do a lot of talking to myself. I have been a widow for a number of years and that has just become a way of making myself feel not so alone, I guess.)

I heard a knock on the door and turned my head to see Anna entering the house to do the first visit evaluation and review with me. I loved seeing her. What an incredible nurse and supervisor, but also a friend. She was absolutely beautiful although her person-ality was not in any way affected by the knowledge of that beauty. She had a way with other people that gave them confidence and hope. And she was so funny! The stories she told were hysterical and you could come away from a casual conversation with her with tears in your eyes from laughing!

Anna had visited the house earlier in the week to prepare a care plan which had been explained to me on the phone, but I had not yet read. Original care plans were left in the home for reference by all, a copy in the file in the office. After introductions between the clients, nurse, and aide, reviewing the care plan together is the first thing to be taken care of when starting a new job. I was so glad she was there so I could share my gut reactions with her later when she left the house, and we could be outside talking as she went to her car. We often spoke to our nurse supervisors at that time when the discussions could be a private matter.

"Hi everyone!" Anna remarked to Ann, Katie, and me.

"Hello, Anna," responded Katie with a smile. "We're looking forward to getting things settled so that we can make sure your people will be taking care of everything we need." Again, I chastised myself quietly.

Anna smiled. "Let's go over the care plan together now that Stella is with us." She went on. "The aides assigned to your home will care for the children as necessary – both those at home all day and the others when they return from school. I believe you told me they got home around 3:00 p.m.?" Anna asked.

"About that time, yes. Sometimes earlier, sometimes a bit later. The bus does stop in front of the house," was the response.

"OK. Caring for the children might entail preparing a snack, helping with homework or perhaps a chore and general activities and supervision. According to the schedule, the aide might do a load of laundry or prepare dinner. Within the time that DYFS has approved, I think the plan will work."

"What about weekends?" I heard one of the ladies ask. She continued. "They can certainly clean the house, then."

I know I winced at that.

In a flash, we all found ourselves looking at each other after we heard a loud crash. Shortly after, a crying child came running into the room. Ann stood up and yelled "Get out of this room. I don't care what happened just now. Can't you see the adults are talking? Go. Go!"

The little girl, Mary, wiped her eyes and nose with her arm, turned around, and ran out.

Anna and I shared glances at Ann's reaction – her deflating, angry words.

After a pause, Anna suggested that perhaps a weekend care plan could be developed independently after the first weekday shifts have been covered with the care plan under discussion. Other hours would have to be discussed and processed by DYFS. Ann and Katie did not look happy with that but shook their heads and said OK. Business was then quickly closed, and Anna said her goodbyes.

I followed Anna to her car. "This might be tough for you," she said. "I will be talking to their DYFS worker about our impressions and worries about the children and how the ladies look to use you and the other aides that will undoubtedly be assigned. The worker told me yesterday that Ann and Katie have asked for early morning hours to get the children breakfast and off to school, as well. We'll see where that goes. If you need help, call me. I am a bit concerned they will try to get you to do work that is not approved. If so, refer them to me and don't make it hard on yourself."

We hugged and she got into her car to drive to another client in the area. I watched her back her car out onto the road where the traffic seemed to be picking up. Maybe teachers were going home.

When I re-entered the house, Ann and Katie had both left the room. I twirled around, thinking, and looking at things; I shrugged my shoulders and went outside to talk to the little ones who were playing. It was almost 2:30 and I had thirty minutes or so to get to know them before the others arrived home.

The three outside ran up to me and asked if I would play a game with them inside. "Of course," I said. I was looking forward to hearing what they had to say about their life with Ann and Katie.

The three ran up the steps ahead of me. The heat was abominable at the top of the stairs. I wondered if the only air conditioning was in the room where they spoke to guests or those who managed the social programs they relied upon for their needs - and money. Another thing I noticed - my cynicism. I sighed and enjoyed the kids' giggles as they ran ahead of me.

I asked that they wash their hands and dirty faces before we played the game and suggested that would cool them off. It worked like a charm and calmed them down a bit. I was shocked when I saw the facilities these kids had. One sink's faucet control was missing so they could not use the hot water. The room was small with a tub and toilet. No shower. Mold was around the bases of the sink and the tub. Thank goodness the toilet had been flushed by the most recent user or I might have had words downstairs. Anyway, the kids finished in the bathroom quickly – and entered their room with their shining faces. Mary and Joey were giggling again. Anthony was solemn.

The bedroom they apparently shared had three single beds set fairly close together, and one large dresser with a broken leg that leaned to the left on the still existing ones. There were no fans and the open windows provided air, but also more heat. Dirty clothes were in a pile in the corner. I wondered how frequently the bed sheets were cleaned. One bed had a few stuffed animals on it. I guessed that was Mary's.

We sat together on the dirty wooden floor and played the game. Mary and Joey sat down on either side of me. Anthony sat across from us. The children were sweet – although Anthony tried to cheat. I laughed to myself, for what child has never tried to get away with something to win a game?

As I look back, I enjoyed the time with these three. They all seemed excited that I was in their room playing with them and they marveled that I sat on the floor! (So did I! I even got myself up!) Mary had a beautiful little smile, that long blond hair, and blue eyes. Her dress, although sporting a few tears and stains, was a beautiful yellow and pink floral print. What a cutie! The boys were both dark-haired with large brown eyes. They had on old worn jeans and t-shirts. Both had sports team logos on their shirts. Anthony seemed the serious one, somewhat brooding and a little bossy. Joey was preciously silly and could not sit still for a second. That aggravated Anthony. I was guessing they were probably good buddies who often fought over trivial things. I thought of my children then and so often during the time I worked in that home. My memories of my young children warmed my heart.

With the rest of the hours ordered for me that day, I enjoyed the little ones for about fifteen minutes more than the game took, then I went downstairs to see what the laundry situation was. There was a new washer and dryer behind an already piled up bunch of dirty clothes. As in the children's room, the floor was bare and dirty looking. A cabinet held the laundry detergent, so I began to remedy the dirty clothes situation. Thinking to myself, I started with the larger sized clothes in case the school children looked as bad as the others when I met them. I was overjoyed to see the new appliances! "Thank you, God," I said aloud.

Need I say that the family was granted the early morning hours, seven days a week. I spoke to the aides assigned to those times when we were at in-services, and they were as upset as me with the whole situation. Ann and Katie rarely got out of bed before the older ones were off to school and barely said, "Good Morning" to the little ones.

The laundry continued to pile up so that was generally the first order of the day for someone; start a load of wash. Laundry, meals, and cleaning were actually being done by the Agency in addition to child supervision, homework and just trying to make the children feel good about themselves. The other aides and I stayed connected and shared ideas that might provide encouragement for the six. I guessed if we had not been there, the children would have had unhealthy food, dirty clothes (I was initially right about the older ones!) and no kind or loving attention. Thank goodness, we had Anna who was personally reporting to DYFS, providing more detailed information than our weekly notes on the back of our timesheets could offer.

One day when I arrived, I saw an exceptionally large tent in the back yard with several adults sitting in chairs next to it. "Oh, my God," I thought. "Who are these people? Friends?" They looked like they were extremely poor and probably homeless. Dirty, rugged looking. I could hear some of what they were saying but could not pinpoint a subject. One of the ladies had a loud, hair-rais-ing, obnoxious laugh and a fondness for the F word. Other children were running around with little Joey, Anthony, and Mary. They wore no shoes, either. I opened the back door and walked into horrid odors of some type of food cooking in the kitchen, I assumed. From my view at that point, I could tell that there had been a bit more mayhem in the house than usual. I wondered when the visitors had actually pulled in and put up their tent.

Ann and Katie walked toward the door and greeted me. "Hi! Did you see our friends out back? They arrived last night. They have nowhere to go, so they will be living here. The kids will have fun, won't they? It will be a little more work for you and the others, so we started a pot of soup for dinner to help out," Ann said. They were both smiling and obviously happy at this recent turn of events. I was stunned. I guess they expected me to thank them for starting the soup. I didn't. They waited a brief moment for me to do so, then shrugged, turned, and walked out of the house toward their friends with the tent. I saw just two additional children at the time. Hopefully, that was all.

I took a private moment to phone the aide that I knew was doing the early morning wake up, breakfast and off to school itin-erary. She answered my call at another client's home whose number I got from the office, so our chat was short. She told me they did arrive in time for her to add a few to breakfast. She also said that getting "our" kids to school when the new ones, as old as they were and not in school, was difficult. As we hung up, I sighed and grew angrier. Talking myself down (now a normal necessity) I decided to take the high road and went about my day, per usual plus five. We decided some time ago to do child laundry only, which was actually a company policy when able adults were in the home. The "adult" laundry pile grew a bit each day until they apparently had no recourse but to do their own.

There were three adults in the new family – two women and one man. They appeared to be around the ages of Ann and Katie. I never learned the details about their relationships with each other, nor their names. Frankly, that didn't bother me. I honestly didn't want to know.

Unbeknownst to me until the next day, the police showed up at the home that evening. Children running into the road, upsetting neighbors and drivers, overly loud music and loud, foul-mouthed adult arguments were all reported by more than one neighbor. This was the beginning of a rather lengthy conflict between these foster parents and the State.

When the aide arrived early the next morning, you might assume that the behaviors would have changed and there might have been some remorse for having the children witness the police visit. Well, no. She told me they were furious about their rights being infringed upon. Katie even emphatically stated that the County may lose some great foster parents and they'd be sorry about that.

In hindsight, the two new children did the others a favor while they were there. They easily noticed the way Ann and Katie spoke to them. We heard it, too, and it was reported to DYFS. Their social worker made visits, but they witnessed nothing that would moti- vate them to remove the children but did provide some parental training classes. I had no idea if that was mandatory, but I don't believe they ever attended.

With the new children talking to the others, Joey, Mary, Andrew, and the older ones started talking back and refusing to do as they were told. This parent-child relationship grew worse as the tent city endured, and everything culminated in two or three weeks of DYFS legal battles with the ladies. They added a dog to the family that incessantly barked and ran through the neighborhood (wouldn't you if you were a dog?) Through it all, the police were called in several more times, and the local newspaper wrote up a story. Of course, Ann, Katie and guests were accommodatingly polite to the reporter, maintained that they received harsh treatment from DYFS and offered a sad story about how cruel the community was to the homeless!

In the end of my involvement with this family, the children were finally removed from the home, the homeless were temporarily provided two hotel rooms and Ann and Katie remained in the house without receiving their large checks from the government. Lizzie was called to the State offices with the DYFS Director to report information and inform them of experiences the aides had while with the case. I never learned what happened to the children. I assumed they had been placed in another foster situation and prayed that it was a happy, clean, and caring home.

During and since my tenure with Ann and Katie's "family," I learned that this was not that terribly uncommon – that people would lie about themselves, fake their sincere desire to provide good homes to foster children, and manipulate the system for the money and the accompanying "perks" like the additional help awarded them by the State. (Ann and Katie hit the jackpot with so many!) Eventually, the truth may become evident but imagine the effects on the youngsters.

Stella

THE SECRETS OF OLD AGE

THE DAY the office called and asked me to see a new client, Ms. Sadlow, I was excited to work with someone new. It was always so uplifting and somewhat spiritual to me to meet and get to know the remarkable people to which we were most often assigned. Their homes, their families, their memories, their personalities, and their knowledge. And, yes, their smiles and their tears. Too often, the tears. I accepted the job, glad that it was wonderfully close to my house, and it sounded like a rather routine scenario. I continued to pray for the six DYFS children I had cared for recently and have thought of their precious dirty faces many times.

Hanna Sadlow was eighty-one-years old. She had been recently discharged from the hospital after a fall. She lived with her one hundred-and-one-year old father who turned the century corner two days before the day that I first met him. I suppose some would say Hanna was a spinster, but as I grew to know the two of them, I realized she was just part of the grand family and would never think of leaving it. Hanna, not her father, Jozef, received the initial Medicare order for six hours a week for two weeks. That didn't surprise me, but overall, he was the one that would need more consistent assistance. I wasn't concerned, though. I knew the Agency would see that service was provided privately to him after the Medicare ran out. The Agency had contracts with the Federal and State governments and additional non-restricted funds that Lizzie could utilize according to need, not strictly financial resources.

Hanna was using a walker and could manage her personal care. I quickly learned that day that Lizzie and Social Services who "knew" the client were working together to fund necessary services for the two as the Medicare coverage expired. I knew Anna would stop by shortly after the service began to acquaint herself with the client and situation. The care plan was prepared by the Medicare Visiting Nurse (VN), but our nurse would inform them of our organization and options of care following the Medicare order.

I was told that Hanna and Jozef lived on a farm. This is a country area and there are many farms around, although over the years the beautiful old stone homes with accompanying outbuildings were being destroyed and replaced with upscale housing. Unfortunately, those born and raised here were unhappy to see the beautiful homesteads taken away and could not afford to purchase any of the new ones. Although a rural county with little to no industrialization, it is ranked in the national list of counties with a high average family income. Large horse farms dot the back roads, interrupted here and there with a private landing strip or horse show arena. Doctors, lawyers, and C-suite employees who work in New York City reside here in the beautifully maintained old estates that had been protected – those where the very wealthy lived during their summer vacations in years gone by.

I was surprised when I pulled into the driveway that day, unaware that it was, obviously, a real working farm! I immediately noted two cows, two goats, a chicken coop with a number of hens and a rooster, and a large garden. I felt as if I had been transported back in time fifty years. The two-story white clapboard house needed painting very badly. Black shutters, equally as old and worn, flanked the windows. The porch covered the entire front of the home, its posts looking sturdy, the floor secure and even. The steps appeared to be sagging a bit, however. The barn was built into a bank, and as barns had normally been constructed, rested on a beautiful stone foundation that extended up the sides of the structure to a midpoint. Boards painted red that were not extremely weathered finished its appearance.

I guess I always assess the physical plant, as it were, of all my new clients before noticing other things that may normally take the eye of others well ahead of the buildings. I am a practical person who lived on a farm in a rural community during my youth and teens. The farmer's work ethic, knowledge of the planting and growth of the crops, and the care of animals is the bulk of required skills and personal traits necessary to have some success as a farming family. The work is difficult and its tasks tiring and demanding. Attention to everything is a daily necessity with little rest from responsibility. The number one pursuit, therefore and always must be, is the protection of self, family, crops, and livestock.

The Sadlow farm was a place full of beauty! The grounds appeared well-kept. The cows looked well cared for and healthy. The pasture in which they were fenced was spotted with green in addition to the expected brown patches and manure piles. An old hay crib – obviously, hand-made - was full of corn silage and some bales of hay had been opened up and strewn around the crib area. Buckets of water were hanging here and there on the fencing. This was a vision waiting to be painted. One of the "girls" started to walk toward the car as I pulled up into a parking area in front of the house. She loudly mooed at me. Not a bleat like a cow can do, so I figured she was just saying "Hello" rather than warning someone of my approach. I smiled and said "Hello" to her. She quietly stood and chewed her cud as I moved along. The curious goats soon investigated me. Both of them were white with brown and black markings here and there. I wondered if they were siblings. I patted their heads and talked to them. However, I really love cows. I spent a good deal of time with them in the summer on the farm where I lived as a young teenager. They were good company for me then.

The day, my first with Jozef and Hanna, was sunny, but a bit on the chilly side as early fall weather was upon us. Overnight chill, but no frost yet. A few of the flowers in the bed which ran the length of the Sadlow porch, just in front of it, showed signs of the rather cold temperatures, but the brightly colored dahlias were blooming and happy in the cool air. Their multi-colored blooms and the autumn tones of the garden coleus blended well through-out. I assumed Hanna had made provisions in her flower garden for blooms of spring bulbs; the harbingers of the season which would signal the end of the winter cold and grey skies. They would be lovely at this place, and I looked forward to seeing them poke through the ground in a few months.

I found the steps to be sturdy enough and knocked on the door. As I waited, I enjoyed the Fall air and, yes, even the smells of the barnyard. The hens were running freely and clucking as they pecked at corn and other feed on the ground. I noticed an old butter churn next to one of the chairs on the porch and admired the attempt at decorating the area. I giggled to myself as I thought of my morning's distress. I had decided that morning to wear my old slacks instead of my newer ones today. I thought to myself as I waited for someone to answer the door that maybe I would be glad I did if they wanted me to do some farm work.

A neat, clean, and proud-looking 81- year-old lady opened the door to me. "Hello. Please come in," she said with a warm smile. She turned to show me the way into a large entrance area. Ahead was a staircase that accentuated the divide on the first floor between the living and dining rooms. I assume a large kitchen and pantry were behind this living area on the main floor like most old farmhouses had been designed.

Hanna seemed to walk rather comfortably using the walker. She had fallen and broken her hip recently while working outside. I knew no specific details. I hoped that she hadn't been on a ladder or something as dangerous. Knowing the farmer in her, I wouldn't have been surprised. The info regarding the hip was helpful to me, though. Knowing that her father, a gentleman twenty years her senior, was living with Hanna, I had wondered why the Medicare order had not been for him.

"Have a seat," Hanna said and gestured to an old, well-used overstuffed armchair. "I am Hanna Sadlow. I live here with my father, Józef, who is napping in the other room just now. You will meet him before you leave today, though. He takes one or two short naps each day. He is 101, you know." She told me about his age with emotion and love in her voice – oh, and pride, too, as she spoke the words "one hundred-and-one" with great emphasis! And that beautiful smile crossed her face again.

We chatted for at least five minutes about her cows, goats and chickens until MK arrived to talk to us. We shared our stories about life on a farm with each other. Good, warm, funny, and sometimes difficult memories.

Our time with MK was pretty routine. Hanna was happy to have the help for a few weeks, although you could tell that she was still going to try to do all that she could by herself. And because everything on the care plan was mainly personal care, I suspected that Hanna was concerned about the needs of the farm and the animals.

While MK was still there, Józef walked slowly into the room. He surprised me and truly did look like an old man who had just gotten up from a nap. There was a good deal of messed up white hair on his head and long, busy white eyebrows that men often get. No beard, but you could tell that he hadn't shaved for a while. What surprised me, though, was the attitude I saw: a little cocky, a little snappy and a well-hidden kidder. I felt like I was looking at a little boy who had a secret on his mind – maybe a young trouble-maker. There was a glint in his eye. Yes, that was it! I saw a little twinkle in this old man's eye. I smiled to myself.

The four of us talked for a few minutes; MK explained to Józef why I was there and told him that other ladies would come at other times as well. We said our goodbyes and I walked MK to her car. "You are going to love these two, aren't you? In all my years in the area, I never knew this farm was here. It's too bad that they can't have the house painted. It is in great shape inside." She went on. "It is obvious, though, that your work will be for both of them since Hanna is obviously Józef's caregiver. You'll need to walk a fine line while it is a Medicare job." Of course, I knew what she meant. You are only to care for the client them-selves, and not others in the home. The client is considered to be homebound and should not be leaving the safety of the house itself unless going to a doctor appointment or rehab. Here I had two people who needed care and the added issue of the farm animals and their needs. I knew I would have to work it out with Hanna. I did some laundry and prepared a meal for them before I left that day.

My visits were scheduled in the morning so the next time I went to Hanna's, I prepared some breakfast. Hanna and Józef both ate well and seemed to enjoy my cooking. It made me feel happy to see that. Then we talked about their needs aside from the care plan and how they felt I could be the most assistance within the plan.

As we began talking, Jozef stood up and walked slowly out of the room. Hanna reached over and touched my arm to get my attention. "He's just going to take a nap. He always needs some sleep after breakfast," she said as she lovingly watched him walk away. I realized that I smiled a lot in this house.

"Hanna," I said, "how can I help you manage the house and farm while you are unable to do the things that you must have been taking care of? Even if you feel up to certain chores on the farm, you are not allowed to do them under Medicare hours. Our organi-zation must obey the rules. I am sure you would want us to. Can you write down the chores and times of day they are to be done? I have to try to help somehow. The Agency might be able to help, too."

"No." Hanna cut me off abruptly (but in a polite tone) as she put her hand on mine. "I don't want the Agency to know how much help we need here. Let's just stick with the plan and I will do the work when you aren't around. That way, no one will know but me!"

"I want to help, Hanna. Please tell me what I can do in the early morning, before my real hours, or later in the day, after the real hours. I will be your volunteer and only you and I will know! Let's figure this out," I said, this time putting my hand on her arm and giving it a gentle squeeze.

"Stella, my father may be 101 years old, but he is a proud Polish farmer. He insists that everything we eat, or drink is from our land and efforts. I buy little at the store. From our cows and goats, we have milk, cream, butter, and cheese. From our chickens, we have eggs and meat. Our garden is large, and I can everything when it is ready so that we have it through the winter. I make jelly and pies from our fruit trees, strawberry plants, and rhubarb in the garden. Father used to fish, but those days are gone. I get to do that occasionally but not often. You have told me that you were raised on a farm. You know what all of this takes." Hanna looked tired, scared and alone as she said these things to me. She wiped tears from her eyes. She took a deep breath and some time to compose herself, sighed, and turned to look at me.

"What are you willing to do on your own time?" There was defeat in her voice then and I would have done anything for them. These were two people who loved and cared for each other more than anything else in this world. Money meant next to nothing. Their selfless pride motivated them to ask truly little in this life. Boy, oh boy, what an uplifting scenario from the one I just left – where irresponsible people took money from the State to take care of children, they cared nothing about, but were paid to parent.

"Thank God there are people like you, Hanna," I said aloud. We talked about what she could do in the house or on the porch and what I could do in the early morning which seemed the best time for me to volunteer. We did not want anyone to know – especially not the Agency.

The next morning, a Wednesday, I went to the house at 6:00 a.m. The Medicare hours were 2 hours each Monday, Wednesday, and

Friday. If I got in the habit of a 6:00 a.m. start there, we would make my volunteer work link to the paid hours. Hanna felt that the additional two hours would be sufficient. She would do the essential chores when I was not there. I hoped that she would not fall.

The first thing I did was to say, "Good morning," to Hanna and Jozef, if he was up, and then I went out to milk the cows and goats. Rainy days were not fun because I could not get the goats to go into the barn, but the cows found their own way in and out of the wet. Cows act on habit and a leader to follow. The girls were easy to milk, and we became friends quickly. The goats were harder to control and really didn't care for me unless I had something to feed them. We worked it out after a while. I quickly gave all of the milk producers nicknames. The lead cow I named Beulah after one that I loved on our farm. The other I named Nellie, and the goats were Martha and Bessie. My Beulah had been very stubborn and always found a way out of the pasture. We never found the hole in the fence. We just shook our heads and walked her back in. Cows are funny. They have this knack of staring blankly at you as they contentedly chew their cud. But they are not dumb. They know when the truck has come to take them to the stockyard. I did too. I hid under the bed so I would not hear their bleating. Thank goodness that was not to be the fate for Hanna's girls.

I took the pails of milk into the house, keeping track of cow or goat variety. Hanna took over from there. On a lovely day, she could churn butter on the porch. (Yep, the butter churn that I saw on the porch was not a decoration.) Days were getting chillier and shorter. We turned the clocks back and the work started in the dark with the lights outside and in the barn, making it all possible. Hanna used the raw milk to make cottage cheese, hard cheese, and butter.

After milking came the feeding of all the farm animals and giving them fresh water. Following that, when the chickens were roaming around and pecking at their breakfast, I gathered the eggs and took them in for breakfast or baking needs. And, finally, the garden had little yet to offer, but some late greens, spinach, and kale, and perhaps some potatoes and onions. So, I would gather them. I thought about the springtime when the planting had to be done and wondered if I could find a friend who would rototill it for them.

When I stayed for my real two hours, I assisted Hanna with her rehab exercises and chores in the house and cared for Jozef. I helped him with his bath, washed his hair and dressed him for the day. He still toileted himself but sometimes had an accident which needed a second round of cleaning up. This always embarrassed him, and he became angry. His brow would knit, and his normally pleasant face would tell of his disgust that I was cleaning him for that reason. I did not speak Polish, but I knew that he must be cursing himself or his old age – or both. It humbled me when I thought of the possibility that someone in a future time would be cleaning feces from my naked old body as well.

Sometimes when Jozef was talkative, we would chat with his broken English while I washed up the floor, folded laundry or made them something to eat. Jozef was a very smart man – knowledgeable about more than farming. He remembered his experiences in Poland to me – including war stories. He spoke about his wife, Hanna's mother, and what a great baker she was. He missed her apple pies, warm out of the oven. He sometimes recalled Hanna's youthful antics when she was not around. He said she was a maciwoda, with a hearty laugh. (Later I looked that up. Our word would be troublemaker.) Listening to him at these times was so delightful and interesting. I thought to myself that he should have authored a book.

I also learned something else about Josef one day. I was looking through a cupboard in the kitchen and moving some of the canned goods around to find the applesauce which Hanna had told me she had put up in the early fall. I thought it would be good to serve Josef with his breakfast. Imagine my shock when I found a number of bottles of a rather colorless liquid. I thought I knew right away what the liquid was. Liquor? Corn, apple, pear? I chuckled to myself and thought this one hundred-and-one-year-old gentleman had a secret to his longevity. I had read about that theory in the paper here and there and in books I had read. When I had a chance to ask Hanna about my find later that morning, she laughed. "You found my father's stash! Corn squeezins! He always has a bottle in his room and takes a swallow every morning when he gets up. He says it makes his day start out right!"

"God, bless his heart," I secretly prayed with a smile. I loved these beautiful hard-working, honest, and loving people.

Our time together was comfortable, warm, interesting, and entertaining. While the work was not always easy, it was pleasant and anything I had to do, I enjoyed doing. Especially when we were in the kitchen working or preparing food, Hanna and I shared memories of our younger days. We spoke about her garden and the flower bulbs that were planted I had not yet seen in bloom. And we laughed, sometimes in giggles like schoolgirls. When Jozef was with us, the words spoken changed somewhat – but his memories were touching and often offered wisdom learned through a long life. His laugh was contagious. I looked forward to my next visit as if these two were my real family.

One morning, MK came to see the Sadlow family as a routine, required nurse visit. It was early and she found me doing the laundry when Hanna welcomed her into the house. Jozef had not yet gotten up, so I was trying to do the non-noisy chores. Thank goodness someone had the good sense to get a washer and dryer into this house. I never asked – I was just grateful.

"How is everything going here?" MK asked as she took a seat at the table in the kitchen where Hanna had brought her. MK always looked the same to me. Neither she nor Anna wore a uniform. MK always wore khaki or navy slacks and a nice top. Neat, but plain. Of course, nurses generally did not wear jewelry for safety's sake. She had taken out a piece of paper to jot important notes down.

"How are you feeling, Hanna? How's the hip?"

Hanna smiled at her. "It's doing OK. I have some pain some-times and occasionally I feel that I need to use a cane...but really good for my age."

MK went on, "How is your father doing? I guess he is doing OK, or I would have heard from Stella."

Almost the exact time MK finished asking about him, Jozef walked around the corner into the kitchen and asked, "Were you able to get them goats milked, Stella?" He did not know that MK was there and perhaps did not know that I was not supposed to be doing the farm chores. Hanna and I both stiffed and looked at each other. (Such telltale behavior!) MK's reaction was purely MK. She calmly asked if I was, indeed, milking the goats. I had to tell the truth. Hanna and I explained that because she needed more help outside than inside, I had been volunteering every morning to take care of the livestock and other outdoor work. I then helped her indoors, as requirements dictated, during my scheduled hours. MK listened and asked a few questions about the work that I was giving in addition to the goats. Out of respect, I told her every detail. Hanna just sat with her hands folded in her lap and listened. Jozef quietly sat and watched us with a somewhat puzzled look on his face.

MK was quiet for what seemed like ten minutes. "Stella, what you are doing is admirable, but not within the scope of the Agency's purpose for your work. You know that. I worry that while you will be doing this – even as a volunteer – you might get injured." She sighed. "Stella, you should have come to us to find help here. If Lizzie finds out, she will release you from this job, if not the Agency. She trains all of you not to get overly involved with your clients – for your sake and theirs. I believe this would come under that category."

"MK," I meekly said, "Without the Medicare regulations, Hanna can start doing some of this work – and more as time goes by with her hip. Please don't say anything to Lizzie! They have to get this work done. The animals know me now. It's no big deal and I won't get hurt. Please don't tell her. It will soon be back to normal here and I can continue to take care of Jozef if a private order is written."

MK stood up to leave. "I will have to tell Anna, but we won't say anything to Lizzie."

The area experienced a difficult winter, but Hanna, Jozef and the animals made it through. Early on, with my help, they had been able to get the financial information together that was needed to apply for reduced fees from the Agency. They never went without service when Medicare coverage was gone. Of course, with the Medicare restrictions out of the way, Hanna managed the care of the animals even through the cold and snow. I continued working with them for quite a while – about six months – before another aide replaced me for understandable reasons. I continued to socially visit with them beyond that.

One day, Hanna phoned me to tell me that Josef had passed quietly during the night. Rest in peace. She assured me that she would be OK. I still drop in occasionally. Approaching her nineties, Hanna maintains her beautiful smile and will probably live to be as old as her father.

Jody

THE BRAVE AND BEAUTIFUL ROSE

I RECEIVED a call from the office one evening to assign a new client to me. The client was bedbound and lived quite close to my house. It was a perfect job for me because she needed four or five hours per day and the hours were split between the morning and late afternoon needs. Close to home and she would be the only client I had. Doing three or four 2-hour clients a day with twenty-minute drives between them often times was difficult. I had a bad back which was bothering me as usual when this call came through. If she were truly bedbound, I would only have to roll her to properly bathe her and I figured I could do that without hurting myself more. The scheduler told me that she had been a client of ours for years and all of the aides really liked her. Even better news! So, I accepted. I started the morning care the very next day.

Rose rolled over a bit in her bed to look toward me as I walked in around 9:00 a.m. I quickly was reminded of her condition as relayed to me on the phone the night before. Rose had been ill for more than ten years. She had been a home health aide for our Agency at one time, so the office knew her and had watched her physical decline over a number of years.

Initially, Rose was independent with a cane, then a walker, then wheelchair-bound and now had been bedbound for almost five years. Rose was also legally blind but worked hard to help herself as much as possible. She could see only slightly better than just moving shadows. The headboard of her bed had built-in shelves that allowed her to conveniently store tissues, meds, and other daily needs. They were well-organized so she could find and pick up what she wanted with no problem. Her phone was also perched there so she could easily pick it up to place it close to where she was lying. She used the phone often and for long conversations. Her telephone had to be dialed by hand. For Rose, the numbers on the dialer were exceptionally large but over time and practice she did not often need the numbers to dial correctly.

Rose also received books on tape from The National Library Service so she could listen to books. One of our aides collaborated with the organization to arrange the service for Rose. She told me she had been an avid reader at one time, so she cherished the opportunity to "read" once again. The tapes arrived and were returned after use through the mail. At the time, it was quite an exciting product and service which is still in existence as books on tape and audiobooks.

"Good morning," she said as she greeted me that first day when I walked into her room. There were a number of windows in the room, but the blinds were closed so the room was somewhat dark, but not dreary. Her face was beaming, and her smile was incredibly unique – sweet but also devilish. She had short, straight, dark hair and her skin looked like that of a thirty-year-old's. She was at least in her late fifties. Sixties, perhaps? I noticed by the bulk under her blanket that she was a large woman and noticeably short. That puzzled me until later when I bathed her. Her legs had muscularly atrophied so much that they had seriously contracted. That morning I was surprised to see her so happy and welcoming. She presented a demeanor that told me she was comfortable in her own skin. "I would not be so jolly if this were me," I thought to myself and I knew that was true. I would probably be anxiously awaiting the end of my life while making everyone else miserable. But not

Rose. No, not her. She taught me about the good life during the time that I cared for her... about fifteen months.

"Hi, my name is Jody," I said as I continued into the room. I reached out to her, and we shook hands. Her grip was stronger than I anticipated.

Rose smiled at me again. "Glad to meet you!" she said. "I assume that you are replacing Becky. The office explained that she was moving out of town. Anita is still working the weekends with me. Do you know her?" she inquired.

I answered that I did. "Most of us get to know one another at the in-services or if we have both cared for the same client. She and I met at the meetings. She is a sweetheart, isn't she?" Rose confirmed my brief description of her.

Rose was a Medicaid client, and I knew that either Anna or MK would be in to go over the care plan with me shortly as required by the State. But I noticed the care plan was on a small table in the room alongside a tablet for the aides to leave messages to each other, the nurses, or the family, so I picked it up and read it aloud. Rose was nodding her head yes to the morning tasks. As we then talked, I began her morning care. Rose was very cooperative and easy to bathe. All of the supplies I needed to wash her were easily available. Her bedroom was part of a small suite that had been added to the home. It had its own entrance door that was useful in years prior. Now, the aides were the only ones to use it.

Rose hadn't left her room in years except for a one-time EMS trip to the hospital. As it turned out, there was no diagnosable problem save a lousy virus that made her temp climb to 104 and her blood pressure lowered to 90/50.

In addition to the bedroom, the suite included a private bathroom where the basin, soap and water were found. I quickly learned that Rose liked to have baby powder sprinkled on her after she was dried. She loved the smell of it, and it truly was a bit easier to get her nightgown over her frame. She was overweight to say it nicely, but who wouldn't be having no real activity for years? With her good arm strength, Rose was able to use a bedpan by herself and when it came to other personal care that I would provide, she could position herself in the bed so that my job didn't require reaching, stress or strain. My job with her was physically easier than I expected. There was little to no odor I noticed with a smile in my mind. Despite her disability, she was clean as was her bedroom and bathroom.

"Does your daughter (she lived with her daughter, husband and teenaged granddaughter) help the aides keep up with cleaning your room?" I asked.

Rose looked up at me as if I had two heads. "My daughter and her family are living their own lives. There are days when I don't see them at all except quick morning and bedtime visits. Peg, my daughter, comes in to unlock and lock the outside door. I know she is disappointed when she sees that I am still alive," Rose said with a laugh.

"What about her husband or daughter?" I asked.

Again, Rose laughed at the question. "I rarely see either one of them. There are times that I hear them yelling at Stacy, their daughter. She is a difficult sixteen-year-old, I guess."

Rose was all cleaned up and in a fresh nightgown when MK came to the door.

"Hi, Rose. Hi, Jody" said MK as she walked into the room via the room's outside door. I noted again that the sun was shining brightly as it opened. I had asked Rose if I could open the blinds to bring in the warm sunlight. She quickly gave her permission now that she was washed and dressed. I felt so sorry that Rose could not enjoy it as the rest of us would sometime that day.

"Hi," we both replied to her about the same time. Laughter.

"Rose is the cleanest one in the room right now." I declared with a smile. "We wanted to be ready to have a chat when you arrived. How are you?" I asked.

"I'm good." she answered. "A-OK at the office and at home. I heard that you gave Lizzie a tough time yesterday, Rose." she said with a grin.

Rose burst out laughing. While shifting her weight to get

comfortable – you wanted to help her, but knew she had to do it herself – Rose told us her Lizzie story.

"Yesterday I called the office and asked to speak with Lizzie. They know my voice so I couldn't play a game by giving an alias. Lizzie answered me as usual. 'Rose, my favorite lady, how are you today?' I had practiced this little prank and so I delivered it perfectly. 'I am so mad and disgusted with your Agency. Lizzie, how could you permit something like this! I always thought you were a good person! The meal was not only late today, but when I opened the meal container, there were roaches inside it! Three of them. What was I supposed to do? I couldn't throw them on the floor and stomp them dead. You know I can't get up and stand, much less stomp! What the hell is going on there? Did every one of your sweet old people who can't make their own meals get these horrible bugs, too? Or worse? You know, there are rumors that Meals on Wheels has served dog and squirrel to us! Tell me, who is funding Meals? I want to file a formal complaint. They need to remove this from your organization and get someone else to run it who is responsible and cares about their clients!"

By this time, Rose was laughing openly and had to pause a bit to gain her composure before completing the story. She continued, "The other end of the phone was completely silent. I couldn't even hear her breathing. No, she wasn't pulling her hair out! No, she wasn't crying. I waited a little bit for her to say something. The longer the silence lasted, the lousier I felt about what I had just done. Finally, I heard Lizzie say, "Rose, not all of our clients had bugs in their meals. Just you. You are also the only one who received dog meat and we only served it once. We have a veterinarian next to us and he needed to clean a carcass. Never squirrel. We were experimenting with the meals and since you were our favorite person, we thought we would give you the honor. I am sorry that you weren't happy. You don't need to file a complaint. The County encourages things like this."

By this time, MK and I were rolling with laughter and then, of course, so was Rose. She had to stop mid-story to compose herself before she could continue to the end. She laughed so hard her face was turning red. I had known she and Lizzie had become phone buddies and Lizzie occasionally stopped for a short visit if she was in the area. But this was hysterical. Typical Rose, I was told.

The three of us chatted for a few more minutes about fun times and good people before we got down to the business of going over the care plan. The three of us agreed that the plan worked well for Rose and her needs.

After MK left us, there did not seem to be much Rose wanted me to do. I sat down, and we talked some more. She told me about her days and what she did to pass the time. I did not know it before, but she not only received a Friendly Visitor from our Agency when she was consigned to her bed, but she was also a Friendly Visitor herself. She had accepted several "friends" and visited with them on the phone. It provided company and uplifting activity to both parties. Rose often spoke to me of these "visiting" phone calls, but never shared any real details regarding health or family problems of others, of course. She would relate general information or stories about pets, problems or concerns about their home and other issues which did not involve any technically confidential information. As she talked and I listened, I increasingly realized how wonderful Rose was. She obviously deeply cared about her phone friends, and I am sure that they felt that warmth through the telephone wires. There was also no doubt that her terrific sense of humor also took the same pathway into their lives.

I often shared myself with Rose, too. She always asked about my husband and two sons. How were they? Did my husband have a new job? He worked on a contractual basis for the State government in cleaning out homes which had become the property of the State by one route or another. These properties were in horrid condition – dead cats or dogs, human filth, vermin running about and piles of trash, broken furniture – you name it. I never knew how he did it. He often traveled into dangerous neighborhoods and never had a problem. He was a tall, athletic guy who had served in the infantry in Vietnam. I guess he just had that "don't mess with me" personae. The money was good, but even more valuable were the treasures he sometimes found. The contract assigned all contents to his responsibility so anything worthwhile was his to take. He also had to leave the home completely empty and dispose of the unwanted contents according to the law. He had to submit the proof that it was handled appropriately. Some days he would bring home a treasure he knew I would love. Paintings, antique jewelry and once ten pairs of my favorite shoes in assorted colors and, thankfully, just my size.

Rose was especially interested in my youngest son, a special needs kid who has a personality that gathers people to enjoy his company. He has an easy laugh and a cheerful outlook that makes every day, every event, and every meal the "best I've ever had!" Years older today than the story I am telling, he remains the same loveable person – a man, now, who has more activities in his life than I do. Rose loved to hear about his Special Olympic opportunities and adventures. He is a swimmer.

As for me, we talked about my hair styles, my struggle with weight loss and my willingness to take in stray cats. I always had long hair, but about that time, I had it cut very short. I didn't have much of it and it was very thin – like a baby's silk tresses. I thought very short hair would not highlight the impending baldness on my head.

Dieting was important for both of us. Of course, she always reminded me that no one saw her fat. I always laughed at this. However, she also reminded me that many, many other people saw mine. I laughed at that, too, but both of us knew the laughter wasn't really legitimate for either one of us. I sometimes found time to read some new diet suggestions in a magazine to her. She played her radio during the day and of course, heard ads for a new wonder pill or the miracles of eating some particular fruit or vegetable. When I tried one of the new diets, she was my sounding board and we kept track of my progress together. Sometimes it actually worked!

To briefly discuss the stray cats here, Rose and I had plenty to talk about. My husband complained about food and vet costs, and I found joy in their purring. We were always at odds, but he had come to love one or two of them over time. Rose wished she could have one, but she knew she couldn't properly care for it. I always had pictures of my cats and one dog to share with her. She was able to see their images to a degree. She looked forward to any new ones.

That first visit with Rose was special, somehow. I wasn't really sure why I already felt as close to her as I had with one or two other clients that I cared for longer than one day, but I did. She was cooperative, easy to talk with and her strength of character despite her life's misfortunes and sufferings was amazing. Before I left that first day, Rose and I discussed the way the total amount of daily hours would be split, acknowledging that morning hours remained most important but may not always need to be lengthier than those allotted in the afternoon/early evening.

One day as I returned in the afternoon I learned more of the truth about Rose and her life; as I walked from my car to the door of her room, I heard a female voice yelling at Rose about how she had ruined the lives of her entire family. I surmised it was Peg and I wanted to slug her.

In two more steps, I was at the door and opening it – my hands clenched in anger and my mind saying to me, be calm, be professional. As I entered, the woman who was yelling looked directly at me and addressed my presence. "Hello! I am Peg, Rose's daughter. You are Jody, aren't you?" she said in a sweet voice with a big smile. "I am glad to meet you. Thank you for caring for my mom!" She stretched out her hand to shake mine. What was I supposed to do?? I wanted to really shake her, not just her hand – but of course, I responded to her gesture with my hand and a fake smile. After the introductions were completed, Peg told Rose and I that she had errands to run and courteously left the room.

When Rose and I could privately speak, I blurted out, "What the heck was that?"

"My daughter's daily diatribe about her feelings toward me,"

Rose answered. "Sometimes she accuses me of pretending that I am unable to get out of bed and walk. Sometimes she just knows I can take care of myself. And, sometimes – most frequently – she tells me that I have ruined her life or Stacy can't stand to look at me. I have learned to appear to her as though I absorb the guilt while I have become completely deaf to it. Otherwise, she would be ruining my life." At offering this final thought, she laughed. I realized it was all that she could really do. She needed the shelter and resources required to physically live comfortably. But mental and emotional needs were obviously not supplied by the homeowner. That's where our Agency came in and I was happy to be a part of that.

Rose had two meals delivered to her at noon that day. One was put into the kitchen refrigerator by the Meals on Wheels' driver to serve as her dinner. We talked as she ate the other one for lunch. As she enjoyed her food, I busied myself with household chores in her room. After she finished her meal and her dessert (always fruit-she was diabetic), I packed up the tape that she had finished earlier in the day in a padded envelope for mailing back to the organization. She had enjoyed the book a great deal. *Rebecca* had been a best-selling Daphne du Maurier tome that Hollywood fashioned into a great movie. I enjoyed the movie. Rose and I talked about it a bit and opened the latest envelope that contained a new book. I slipped that tape into the player. It was *Breakfast at Tiffany's* by Truman Capote.

It was hard for me not to talk to my family about Rose. Trying to only tell them about the woman, I kept information about her family interactions and their treatment of her to myself. After all, I was proud to know her and spread the word about the lady who ably turned suffering into happiness for herself and others.

While I was with her, perhaps doing laundry or other chores that prohibited consistent talking to each other, Rose sometimes made her Friendly Visitor calls to someone she had been assigned. You could always tell that the conversations were either interesting, fun, or emotional. I knew when, at the other end of the line, there was loneliness, anxiety, or grief. Rose seemed to speak a lot less and when she did, she spoke comforting words. Sometimes she offered verses from the Bible she had memorized. That always moved me because her faith was strong, and her situation was so difficult. I thought to myself that she and my son would be among the most welcomed in Heaven.

Rose had attended the same church for many years – I believe dating back to her teen years perhaps? When she became unable to attend services, they began dialing her just before the service began and with two opened phone lines, she was able to experience the event from her bed. I doubt that she ever missed a Sunday. She and the pastor enjoyed personal phone calls often. Sometimes when I was there, I was privy to her end of one. She was a treasured gal in her congregation. When I think of this today, I wonder how much more she would have felt a true part of the group with the current technology.

Back to the story of her family and how she was treated.

As I have mentioned, the teenaged granddaughter's name was Stacy. Rose told me of several "trials" with her, but I was also around when one or two of them broke out.

"I am not staying home. I am going to Pete's place, and I don't care what you say, you bitch," I heard Stacy screaming at Peg, I assumed.

Rose and I glanced at each other and then faced the door into the house again as if looking at it helped us hear the argument going on behind it. "You are grounded for the shit you pulled last weekend and you are not leaving this house!" retorted Peg. Having experienced the nice and not so nice façade on that woman, I could imagine what it looked like then. I almost laughed. "And that Pete is nothing but trouble for you."

"You don't even know him," screamed Stacy. Peg's voice grew even louder. "If he is such a nice guy, why don't you meet him at your house?" she shouted. "Why doesn't he come here?"

Stacey apparently punched the wall in real anger because we heard a loud thump near the door. "Because I don't want him here.

I don't want him to know – or even see – that freak in this room here. If she were gone, we could have someplace to go to. But, no, that freak has to be here! In our house, the bitch. Why the hell do we keep her?"

It took a split second for me to emotionally respond to this. I turned and looked at Rose. She was white as snow although her cheeks were flushed, and tears were slowly falling down them and running onto her chin. She didn't bother to grab a tissue. I was stunned to watch someone so dear being hurt so badly by someone who should have at least respected her, even if she didn't really like her, for God's sake. It was quiet in the room momentarily as we both realized that it was also quiet in the hallway behind the room door.

"I guess Stacy went out." I said as I broke the silence. "Peg must have given up."

I went over to Rose and held her hand. "I am so sorry you heard that," I uttered. Tears were welling up in my eyes as well. I admit I wanted to physically hurt both of the women. I did write this up in my daily notes for the nurses on my time sheet, but my note was short. Rose heard her niece and daughter angrily arguing outside her room door. Nothing could be done, really, I thought with a sigh.

Peg's husband was no different than the two ladies when it came to Rose. His problems here were a bit different, however. She cost him money. He could have rented that room and bath. He was paying for her electric and telephone bills. He has to bring dinner to her when Peg prepared it on the days when Rose does not order two lunches from Meals on Wheels. He once told me he hated going into her room because he never knew what he would find there. Perhaps she pooped in the pan and the odor was bad? He would never empty that. Never. And what if she was dead? He acknowledged he wished she were dead after that comment. Rose told me it was the same when Peg brought dinner to her. No conversation at all. She put the food tray on Rose's lap tray, turned around and left. I could not imagine living full time in this sad and angry family environment. And Rose smiled and provided encouragement and solace to others that were aged, confined to home, and lonely.

I will never forget one particular afternoon that I worked with her. We had, again, for the hundredth time that morning talked about the problems with my hair and how I should wear it. We agreed it was best very short, but certainly not very sexy. And I didn't wear makeup, either, which bothered her. "Your husband deserves a beautiful gal to greet him after a hard day's work," she would say to me. "I always tried to look my best for my man." She had been happily married until her husband was killed in an accident.

When I arrived the next day, she smiled and said to me, "Do I have a surprise for you!" She held up a beautiful deep brown wig – long hair with soft curls. The bangs were styled to sweep across the forehead. "Come here. Come here!" she sang out as she waved her hand to come to her side. "Here, sit down so I can put this on you!" she chirped; her smile as big as it could get with a giggle caught in her throat!

I sat down on the side of her bed with my back to her. She slid herself up in the bed a bit to access the two pillows that were there which she could lean against for support as she reached up to place the wig on my head. With my short hair, there was nothing to tuck under the wig that wasn't already covered by it. I immediately thought I was not going to be able to stand it. I had never had my head covered like that – even winter hats leave space for your head to breathe. "For goodness' sake. Relax! It's just a wig," I told myself. "Oh, my goodness," Rose shrieked. "Turn around and let me see you!"

I stood up and turned around anticipating hearing her break into a laugh! Instead, I heard her saying how beautiful she thought that I must look with the long hair. I rushed into the bathroom to look in the mirror at myself; again, anticipating a laugh – but mine this time. "No shit!" I found the words loudly popping from my mouth.

"Rose, this looks fabulous. I am a new person. I should be in the movies," I marveled as I turned my head from side to side admiring not only the soft curls, but my own face, as well. I was stunned. Then I heard Rose laughing. She was laughing because I was so happy.

What a warm, loving episode that was between the two of us. I often think of the unselfishness of the lady. She wanted me to look gorgeous and sexy for my husband. The man in my life that I would drive my car home to. The man who I would cook dinner for and who would hold my hand while we sat on the couch and watched a movie together. Rose's life had none of those things and yet, she wanted things to be even better for me. I asked her once where she got the wig. It had been one that she had purchased for herself and her husband. The other Aide, Anita, had located it for her.

I could relay the many talks and happenings that we experienced together. The love of her "books" and the rundown of the plots as they unfolded to the reader were shared with me almost daily. In fact, I had been a voracious reader for much of my life, but for years, I had not turned a page except in the newspaper or the occasional magazine. Rose's love of the story motivated me to pick up some good reads that I had in my house. I am now a member of the local library.

She asked me to help her with the Friendly Visitor role in her life. Together we sent Get Well, Happy Birthday and Thinking of You cards to the many she knew. She gathered the information – addresses, birthdays, etc. Aides and staff would donate the cards, giving them to me at in-services. I would address the envelopes and Rose would write a note and sign the inside of the cards. We split the cost of postage. I thought that was fair and it really didn't add up to too much per month. I was able to keep her window clean and washed and dried her drapes periodically. She loved the sun and that window faced south. Not only did it brighten her days, but when the sun shone into her room in the winter, it provided good warmth. At Christmas, we sang carols together as I cleaned her room or helped her bathe. I have a beautiful lace doily that she gave me one year. I usually gave her baby powder, scented soap and/or cashew nuts (her favorite). Oh, and we always discussed the recent show of our favorite soap opera. Sometimes when I was there in the early afternoon for a specific reason, we watched our "soap" together. That was easy to do when I was managing other tasks. Funny when two people who have watched their "soap" for years get together and talk about the characters. The conversation can get pretty emotional.

There were many times when I would bring my son to visit with her. They had so much fun together. He was always happy and excited to tell her about work or his swimming. Once he visited with me following his return from a State swimming meet where he won a gold medal! He talked up a storm to poor Rose as he told her about his experience.

I was getting ready to leave the house one early fall morning when the phone rang. It was the office calling to tell me that Rose had passed away during the night. Peg had phoned to inform us.

My heart actually broke, I think. It was a horrible thing, yet I was happy for her. She was surely in Heaven and had a whole new body. She was surrounded by love.

Rose was cremated and her ashes were buried in the flower garden by the front door of her church. Lizzie, Anita, and other aides stood with me through the ceremony, a certain celebration of a beautiful life.

Lizzie

GOOD EATS

I WAS BLESSED to have the good fortune of hiring employees who were team players and happy to pitch in where help was needed. It didn't matter what service or what "department" of the Agency, whatever was needed always enticed a volunteer or two to step up to the plate. We were always very busy, which meant precious minutes or longer had to be taken from their responsibilities to change the direction of efforts and run out of the office for a time; the necessity of immediate responses generally came from the Meals on Wheels program.

Meals were served at three Senior Centers where the food was also packaged for delivery in that specific area. Unlike the aides, volunteer drivers did not have the opportunity to know their lunch guests well. Although the lady or gentleman wanted to talk to the delivery person, there was no time to give, other than a quick "Hello and how are you?" That exchange may have occurred while the volunteer was opening the meal containers for the client. Other meals were waiting in the car that needed to be delivered while they were still hot and/or cold. Hot packs and ice packs were always needed for the food required to meet FDA regulations. Hot meal and/or soup versus salad, milk, and dessert or fruit.

Very few volunteers complained about the work they were doing or time they gave. We hosted a lovely annual luncheon for all volunteers for a few years until their numbers grew into the hundreds. Our Board members at the time called the event a "Tea" and prepared food akin to high tea offerings (little finger sandwiches and desserts), located at one of their homes. They would work for two days preparing the food and the rooms for the event. Tables and chairs were rented, linen tablecloths pressed and spread on each. Between the Board members, an adequate number of silver tea pitchers were gathered and polished to their original gleam accompanied by sugar and cream containers. Earl Grey was served as well as a coffee offer. Several ladies made cream cheese and cucumber finger sandwiches in large quantities. Another group made egg and tuna salad sandwiches. Both groups used different types of bread for each type of filling – all crusts were cut off first and bread squares were cut into four triangular pieces. Desserts were not just brownies or cake. Madeleines and mini eclairs were made by a third group of lady bakers. On event day, the atmosphere was lovely and special. Fresh flowers adorned each table as well as the coffee and dessert area. The sandwiches were presented on china plates. Background music was low - usually sounds of Sinatra and others from that era.

The very special outcome of this day was not only acknowledgement of good works, relaxation, and enjoyment of food made of thanks and love – it was the coming together of the organization's "aristocracy" and those that spread the mission of it; providing good news to the area residents, regardless of age or need.

At one such event, I noticed a young, tall, handsome man had joined us. He stood out like a sore thumb among the many elderly persons – mostly women and a few men. I inquired of one of the site managers who he was and learned that he was volunteering to deliver meals routinely, he was responsible and could be relied upon, and he was a CPA. I thought to myself, "A Godsend!" I asked the site manager to grab him up for us – which she did, and he became very involved on our Board and a tremendous asset to the organization. When the numbers became too large to finance the luncheon and our Board "personality" changed with the coming on of younger members who held jobs, we no longer hosted the "teas" and relied on thank you notes and small gifts to acknowledge the volunteers' amazing work.

It was when illness or severe weather came around and the drivers for that day let us know that they were not going to deliver the meals, phone calls went out to other routine volunteers who were off that day or to those who were contacted over the office intercom. There were many times I was the one who answered the intraoffice cry for help. I was never unhappy to take the time. Depending upon the particular Center from which the help was requested, there may have been six or more routes of ten or more stops each.

When I was asked to take a delivery route, I had the opportunity to talk to our employees and clients and observe how the Center was being run and the overall job was being handled. That was very helpful to me in that I was inadvertently given time to take care of administrative duties away from the office. Sometimes I felt imprisoned in the office for ten hours a day with so many other tasks and issues at hand. I was able to observe the packing of coolers, the serving of the food for the Center guests and sample the food. Rarely was there a whole meal left, so on the way back to the office, I bought a fast-food lunch for myself which did not happen often. It was a treat.

I must admit I remember one specific time when I was not altogether happy to fill in. Two of us from the office went together to deliver that day. The snowstorm had come without warning, and we had no notion of closing the program earlier that day. We had to take the food that was already prepared by our caterer and loaded on their vehicles, and we had insufficient time to alert our clients that we were not going to operate. We generally issued radio and TV notices by 4:00 a.m. on the morning of shut-downs due to a weather alert. This day, we were between a rock and a hard place. We had the food and we had to deliver it.

Pam sat in my passenger seat while I was driving. She was willing to get out of the car and deliver the food to the front door. I can still close my eyes – years later – and see the roads and the visible ice that covered the snow on the roads. In this rural county, the cities got the ploughs immediately because no farmer was going to wander to the grocery or hardware store that day. I was actually shaking as my car slid here and there as if I were turning the wheel slightly, side to side. I occasionally did this in time to the music I was enjoying as I went down a clean, dry, lightly traveled road. But this was not the case that day. It was nasty to say the least. To make things worse, my sight was often blurred by the intensity of the storm as the wind blew in heavy spurts. Pam and I barely talked as we completed the run that day. While the wheels were turning, our focus was just on what was ahead. She was able to walk to the front doors without shoveling and the car did not get stuck to the point of no return. I had to work on getting good traction by rocking the car back and forth once or twice, but always made it to the next stop. I guess my surreal remembrance of the event was because of the stress I experienced for our safety and the clients that day. But I also remember the paradoxical beauty of the falling white flakes that were coating the trees and sparkling on the ground. I love snow.

There were four Senior Centers in the county. It was a large county which demanded a willingness to use both the drivers' time and gasoline to be a delivery person. There were buses that were available to take the seniors to the Senior Centers free of charge. The Centers served lunches – plated portions of the same food that was otherwise packed in containers to go to shut-ins throughout the County. The Center Managers also provided educational opportunities, entertainment, and just plain socialization for the attendees. Many became good friends, and many became involved as volunteer friendly visitors or respite care workers, both managed by MJ.

The entertainment at the Centers was quite diverse. Perhaps today a pianist from their own group and tomorrow the Agency's nutritionist to discuss their "food health". Next week, a dance instructor or a clown may come along to provide exercise and laughter. Card and board games were popular and as both were available at all times, a deck may be shuffling in the corner before the meal was even served. The Centers were very popular, but we kept an eye on census so that we understood our value and how to change or improve it to meet the needs or wants of the current elderly population.

Aide, Jody, was a member of the clowning organization in the area. She and I worked up a skit to represent the many "wonders" of our organization and how the services became valuable as a person aged. I, dressed as a clown, pretended to be the "person" and Jody, dressed as a very buxom nurse with uniform and cap, pantomimed the person in stages of aging and as the needs increased, I climbed a real ladder to the top. We took our show to all of the Centers. I believe we enjoyed it more than our audiences. The picture of me, still in costume, but sitting at my office desk remains, proudly framed and in view, in my house.

So many clients became well-known by drivers and Center personnel, both by experience and through stories others would tell. One lady lived on the first floor of an apartment building. There was an apartment entry that opened to a narrow driveway leading into the parking lot. The drivers loved to deliver to Corny, apparently a nickname that stuck with her from years before. She would watch through her window for the car to approach, then open the window, hail the driver who would lower their window and pass the food through to her. She was always happy to greet the driver with a big smile and a "Hi" before sharing a few words. She could brighten the day.

There was another lady – on that same route - who greeted you at her front door. She always looked like she had a party to attend or maybe a date? Her hair was styled, and she wore a clean, pressed outfit; she wore a skirt and blouse or lovely dress it seemed every day. Through the opened door, you could see into the dining room. There sat a dark wood oval table and four chairs. The table was draped with a pink linen tablecloth. On it was a table setting for one. A pink linen napkin under the silverware sat on the cloth at the far end of the table from the front window which faced the street. Two silver candlesticks with eggshell-colored candles adorned the center and on occasion, they would flank a floral centerpiece. I marveled at that woman. Was she humble and just respectful of civil living or arrogant with a wealthy, spoiled background? I always chose to believe the former. I never got to know her other than "Hello," and "Thank you."

The nutrition program clients – either in the Senior Centers or those who received deliveries – were of varied personalities and lived such different lives from one another. Some like the pink linen tablecloth lady were proud, worldly persons who apparently had comfortable situations, some were well-educated, and some dropped out of school to work, some had spouses and children while others only had their memories. There were those who lived in poverty, alone and lonely and those who lived alone with canine and/or feline friends. The latter always brought attention to themselves. Those in the center brought pictures of their dogs and shared them with others. They became like their children in that you would hear someone ask, "How is Rosie feeling today?" Rosie was often a pet.

We were generally aware of those who had their meals delivered, were alone, and had a pet. When one of our Meals on Wheels clients was away from home, in the hospital or deceased, we were normally informed to discontinue their meals. But sometimes, that did not happen. If they were hermits, as such, we often did not know until we tried to deliver the meal. We occasionally had to have the police knock down a door and find someone who had fallen, who was deceased, or someone who had obviously left their home to go to the doctor and forgot to inform us. A lady not far from our office was one of the fallen. We called 911 and the ambulance arrived to pick her up. It was a bit inconvenient for the meals that remained to be delivered. Because it was close by, the Manager of Meals on Wheels, Darlene, left the office and stayed with the client so the volunteer could continue with their route.

Darlene stayed connected with me and informed me that the client was being taken to the hospital and she would lock up and return to the office. She returned to work with an adorable older dog who came in and found a place to lie down and take a nap. Darlene took her home that evening and kept her until her "mother" was discharged and returned home. Meanwhile, the team took turns caring for her at the office during the workdays.

We lived in such different times then, but they were always interesting.

Charlotte

MUCH LIKE A FAMILY

I LIVE in a small but lovely little house on Main Street in one of the County's downtown areas.

I lived a comfortable life until two deaths in my family almost destroyed me. My daughter died in her early twenties of cancer and only two years after, my husband, Jerry, succumbed to a stroke. I was in mourning for over a year – feeling cheated and lonely. I was angry, too. My only saving grace was my job as a Home Health Aide. With it, I eventually felt worthy of a new life if it presented itself. And, through it all I also learned more about my clients and what they were dealing with: pain, confusion, questioning, doubting, and in general, loss. When someone dies, you don't just lose them. You seem to lose your sanity, your confidence, your purpose in life and a part of your identity. My empathy for my people became more real and much deeper.

I am a tiny lady and not a spring chicken. When I was asked to care for a post-stroke patient who lived with her husband almost around the corner from me, I hesitated to take it. Would I physically be able to manage her bathing, diaper changing, and other vital physical needs? As I thought it over, I reflected on the fact that I could easily walk to work. It was a safe town so heading home after dark would be safe, after all. I also needed the money I would earn working eight to ten hours a day, five days a week. It would be very worthwhile. I decided to accept the job and if I couldn't provide the needed physical assistance, I would ask to be replaced.

Sam and Meg had been married for thirty-five years. She was just fifty-five when she suffered the stroke that left her with little functioning of her body. It was as if she was a young child. She did not speak but was able to communicate somewhat with grunts, mumbles, and a sound like a mild scream. Gratefully, she could still laugh. Meg recognized her husband and others she came to know through frequent contact. She also understood what you said to her, especially when it referred to her activities and needs. Bath, lunch, roll over and other requests were not just recognized, she reacted appropriately to them. That was the saddest part – she knew what was happening around her and was able to participate to a certain degree. I pitied her.

If there was one bright and certain thing in her life, it was her husband. Sam loved her with all his heart. He held an excellent job and at his age he could not retire. Thus, my hours with Meg covered his workday so he could keep her in her own home – with him. They had no children, so each was the world to the other.

When the scheduler called me about doing this case, I learned that it was not under Medicare or Medicaid. It was a private client. I shivered inside when I did the math. Forty or fifty hours a week times our organization's private fee equaled a great deal of money. Realizing this, I felt even worse for Sam who had to earn that plus ordinary living expenses. His road had to be hard mentally, emotionally, and physically. What time could he possibly have for himself? What pleasure?

I started my first day of service at eight o'clock in the morning. Sam answered the door with a "Good morning" greeting to me and a smile on his face. He was appropriately dressed for his day at work; he had a desk job in a sizeable company and wore a suit and tie each day. He showed me into the living room to sit and talk for a bit. I remember I was anxious to meet Meg, wondering if I could even do this job properly without putting myself in harm's way. If I hurt myself doing my job, there might not be any more jobs. I needed a purpose in life and a way to spend my days productively.

After I noted the suit he wore, I realized that Sam was quite a good-looking man. It was obvious he was not of retirement age, but I thought he was probably in his late fifties or maybe just over the sixty mark? He was average height for a man. Not thin. Not heavy. His dark hair was peppered with grey. His complexion that morning, despite his smile, was a bit ashen. I thought to myself that he was tired or stressed. Or it could possibly be both? I certainly would be.

We each took a seat in the living room. It was a lovely, neat, and clean room. I admired a number of the decorations and pieces of artwork hanging on the walls. Meg must like color, as blues, pinks, greens, and yellows worked together throughout – both on the furnishings and wall art. To think they were enjoying each other's company sitting there together just a brief time ago.

"Thanks for taking us on," he said as he opened the conversation between us. "I appreciate your ability to help us on a regular basis. Meg is basically easygoing although she has her spells when she yells out and behaves stubbornly. She also cries sometimes. I so wish we could know what is inside her head – you know, what she is thinking. I believe she cries because she is aware that she is in a type of prison without possibility of escape. It must be so very difficult for her." His own tears had welled up in his eyes as he talked to me that morning. As the months passed, he still cried when he occasionally spoke of her prison.

He asked about me. I told him I had been with the Agency for about ten years and enjoyed my job. I went on to say that I had met so many wonderful people through the years that I had been caring for others in their homes.

We both ended the conversation abruptly and turned our heads as we heard the knock at the door. I was happy for the timing because I didn't want to share my personal sorrows with him that morning. Or maybe, never. I heard MKs voice as Sam opened the door.

MK had been to see Meg and assess the situation the day prior to my arrival. She had prepared a care plan according to "day" and "general time frames" because it was such a comprehensive effort five times a week. The three of us went over the basics of the plan. Of course, with my experience, none of the tasks listed were anything that I had never done before. There was a combination of personal care for Meg, cleaning, laundry, and food preparation. We discussed a few loopholes that came to mind that had to be confronted, like who would do the grocery shopping or run certain errands which would take the caregiver out of the house for a span of time. Luckily, there was a physician and a dentist who had agreed to see Meg at her home. Both practitioners also served a nursing home nearby, so they understood the desire of keeping Meg home as long as possible. Sam had arranged for the local grocery and drug store to make deliveries to their home as needed. I never knew if this was kindness or if he had to pay for the services, but it certainly was a tremendous help to him.

After reviewing and discussing the practical side of things, we went into the bedroom to see Meg. While discussing my role in this home, I became almost bonded to a certain extent. I felt somehow, I would be helping my husband if he had lived through his stroke. My heart made me feel like it was my duty and one I was happy to undertake. However, I remained worried that I could not physically manage the requirements of the job.

Meg was awake as we walked into the room. At first, she had a look of fear on her face and then she noticed Sam and smiled a smile that warmed the room. She made a mummering sound as he walked toward her to lean down and kiss her on the cheek.

Meg was not a large woman; I was happy to see that considering the personal care I would be giving her. She wore her hair short for easy management. It was raven black, shiny, and healthy looking. That surprised me because her skin was pale, wrinkled, and had a dehydrated look. However, that beautiful hair told me she had been receiving loving care. "Sam must be doing that," I thought. "Message to self: Make certain she gets enough fluids through the day."

"Meg, this is the nurse from the Agency," said Sam. "They call her MK. The other lady is Charlotte. She is your aide who will be here to take care of you and do home chores Monday through Friday while I am at work." Meg seemed to understand. She murmured again.

When we left Meg and went back into the living room, I told Sam and MK about the anxiety I felt regarding physically handling Meg. Sam assured me she would help and respond to my requests. We talked a bit more until the three of us had an agreement that if I continued to be uncertain about my safety or that I might hurt Meg, the Agency would replace me. I sighed a sigh of relief. It was around nine o'clock that morning when both Sam and MK said their goodbyes and I was left to begin my time in the care of Meg.

When I walked into her bedroom, she seemed calm and, did I see a bit of a smile? "I'm back, Meg." I looked at the care plan briefly, then looked at her. She was watching me.

"Let's drain your catheter bag and then give you a bed bath. Is that OK with you?" She mumbled. I guessed that meant that she was fine with it. Sam told me that everything I needed for her personal care was in the bathroom. I found a container that was being used in which to drain the urine. The process was easily accomplished but I remembered that we did not discuss the changing of the catheter or who would help when it was clogged. I was not allowed to do that. Maybe Sam changed it to a routine schedule? Another message to self: "I have to remember to ask him about catheter care when he returns from work this evening."

The bath went easily. Meg rolled from one side to the other when I asked. She seemed to like the water temperature, but I wasn't sure. When I asked if it was too hot or too cold she did not react either way. I learned to regulate it the way I liked it. In the future there was never a problem with that.

After bathing, drying, and putting a clean diaper and nightgown on her, I brushed and fooled around with her hair so that it looked styled. She had a natural wave that was easy to show off. I also moisturized her skin and massaged her shoulders in the process. She mumbled at that. While bathing her, I looked for any sign of skin breakdown and noted none. I also checked her feet and noted her nails had recently been trimmed. Sam, I guessed. Note to self, "Ask him. Let him know that I am not allowed to do that, either."

I prepared lunch for Meg – chicken sandwich with no more than a tablespoon of mayonnaise and an apple that I peeled and cut into small pieces. I had to feed her, but she was able to chew and swallow the food in small bites. She ate well. While she napped after eating, I tidied up the house, did a load of laundry, and vacuumed here and there. I also wrote a note or two on the tablet provided for communication, even though I would speak to Sam before I left. I would write a bit more on my time sheet.

Although there was routine housework, the day seemed awfully long to me that day. How do I spend my time?

As the next few days went on, I learned to adjust to the schedule that was best for Meg. I continued to do her personal care, move her legs and arms with pared down range of motion exercises, see that she had food and sufficient liquids to keep her hydrated and sat with her to keep her company. But the days remained long, and as I sometimes watched the clock on the wall in the living room, I was already regretting taking the job. I felt rather guilty as that weariness of my work entered my mind. When it did, however, I focused my thoughts on poor Meg living as she did and her loving husband having to work hard to take care of her and to pay the Agency for my time. Those mind images generally woke me up to the reality of my purpose.

That particular evening when I went home after speaking to Sam about the day, I talked to myself about my attitude. If Jerry had lived, what would I think of someone who helped him after his stroke and was treating him as I was treating Meg? Would I have thought that they were selfish? Self-centered? A bad, unfeeling person? "Yes, yes, yes," I answered my own questions that raged through my mind. "So, OK. What do you do to adjust this attitude and have greater empathy for Meg? How do you treat her with respect as if she were her normal self?" I was thinking faster now – focused on the one thing that mattered – how I felt about Meg and how could I help her fill her days? Wasn't she lonely? Like Sam said, "locked up in a prison...." Don't get me wrong. I felt empathy for both Meg and Sam, and I was gentle and wanted to do my best to make Meg feel good. The problem was not really me, I thought, but the length of time I was there. Would I have reacted the same way to a member of my family or someone who had a bad case of the flu? Boy, did I do soul searching. I was a great caregiver for years. But now, I was stymied.

The next evening when Sam came home from work and after he went to see Meg and kiss her hello, we sat together in the living room and talked "off the clock."

"Sam, I am wondering how I can fill my days here to continue being of help to Meg and to you after the routine care is given and household chores taken care of. I like to cook and bake. Is there something I can make for the two of you? I can make you dinner every evening. What kind of books did she used to read? I can read to her. Does she like to listen to music? What do you think?"

"I didn't think about your day this way," he replied. "Thank you for bringing this up. I would be pleased if you prepared us dinner. Then we can enjoy it together – one forkful for Meg and one for me. He smiled and laughed a quiet laugh. We like everything. Perhaps you leave me a list of what is needed at the grocery store, and I will have it delivered. As far as reading and music. Let me see," he said as he thought. "She likes mysteries. And she likes all types of music - instrumental to opera and current hits. She also likes Sinatra, Dean Martin, and the like. Big Bands," he continued to think. "You can find those types on the radio by her bed. I think that would please her," he continued. "Maybe the stimulation she needs to keep her alive in her own head," he pondered aloud.

I said my goodbyes and went home that evening with thoughts

rushing through my mind. I started a menu for the following week before I went to bed. "You have a new purpose now," my mind and my heart said to me.

The next day was a Friday. I had a decent library of books in my house. Both Jerry and I had been avid readers for years. I looked over the shelves full of hardbound and paperbound stories and located a good mystery novel, the first of Sue Grafton's alphabetized series – *A is for Alibi* in which she introduced her famous detective, Kinsey Millhone. I remembered my husband enjoyed reading it, so I slipped it in the bag I was taking to work which included the menu and the list of needed products for the following week. I also took a boxed brownie mix that I could make that day.

As the days and weeks followed, more routine fell in place intermixed with the uplifting and productive efforts I initiated that day. Meg lit up like a lightbulb when I walked into her room in the morning followed by smiles given to me throughout the rest of the hours we were together. I found myself in the second Grafton book, *B is for Burglar*. Meg appeared to listen and sometimes slept while I was reading. Occasionally, she would grunt or smile at something I read, so maybe she understood more that I realized. That would be wonderful! When I left her room to do chores or to prepare dinner, I turned her radio on so that she could enjoy the company of music that she liked.

One morning I found myself in pain as I reached out to wash her back and backside. She had rolled over on the other side as always, but my own back said, "Not today!" That was a surprise and a big annoyance. I had recently purchased a new nightgown for her at a thrift shop. It was in its original packaging and had never been used. The print was one of lively colored flowers and it sported lace on the bodice. I washed it the night before and was going to surprise her with it that day. I pulled myself together, thinking that I had an Advil in my purse, finished her bathing, and put on her new gown. She murmured and grunted and smiled all at once, I think. She was so happy! I could hardly wait for Sam to see her in her new dress.

By the time Sam came home that evening, I was under the influence of the pain pills – I remember taking three – and seated in the living room. The dinner for the evening was mostly prepared. All that needed to be done was to cook the frozen vegetables.

"Are you OK, Char?" Sam inquired with a look of concern across his face. He had a furrowed brow look.

"Of course," I replied, "I am fine. My back just hurts a little bit. It will be fine tomorrow."

He didn't accept my answer and went to his phone to call MK. "I am calling your nurse. She can help here." And so, he did. I was so embarrassed when MK knocked on the door just a brief time later. She had conveniently been visiting a client who lived practically across the street.

"What's up, Charlotte?" MK called out as she entered the house. "My back hurts, but I will be OK. It's a temporary thing, I am certain," I responded.

The three of us talked about the situation. I related the day's work. Finally, I admitted that the problem had been growing. My back seemed to be in spasm while I was there, but it calmed down at home. When I woke in the morning, it always seemed to be fine.

MK turned to Sam. "I believe getting a hospital bed for Meg would help. Charlotte is repeatedly doing what I call half-bends while she is caring for her. The hospital bed could be raised so that she wouldn't have to often be in that posture."

MK and I both awaited Sam's response. I assumed that he would say, "OK. Let's do that." But he didn't.

"Do hospital beds come in doubles?" he asked. MK and I were taken by surprise. Then we both realized he continued to sleep beside her. I never considered that as I did the laundry and other chores. He was still sleeping with Meg to comfort her.

"No, I don't believe so," MK replied.

"Then we can't do that. There must be another way," he remarked as he went into see Meg and kiss her hello. He had been home for some time and had not yet gotten to see her.

I recall looking at MK and her return expression to me. We were both amazed that we hadn't realized this before. I don't really know exactly why this was a little strange to me, but it was. I guess it was for MK, too. But she was also thinking. When Sam returned to continue our conversation, MK told him that it is possible for him to raise their bed using pillar-type supports that he could purchase.

Sam purchased the supports. MK, and MKs husband, helped Sam pick her up and hold her while Anna and I put the supports under the bed's legs. After the supports were installed, Meg was placed back into her bed. It was somewhat frightening at first, but it was a sturdy fix and met the need. It also worked to relieve my back pain and keep me from hurting anymore for the duration of my service to them. Meg was not aware of any difference in her life. Losing her husband's arms would have been tragic for both of them. Regardless of our experiences, there are still so many things we do not realize about the value of love, devotion and simply being human. I cried that night. I missed Jerry terribly.

Weekends had been a personal problem for me. Going out alone was no fun. Grocery shopping was easy. But I shied away from other activities. As I got to feel more comfortable alone, I went to the movie theater where there was something I thought I might like. I drove through the county back roads to enjoy the scenery and even stopped for lunch while in a small town I had newly discovered.

I always thought I had deep insight into myself, but I realized I actually did not. I was afraid to be alone. But why? After I lost my immediate family, much of my identity disappeared. Yes, I was still a working woman doing good things in my community. Yes, I owned a lovely little house. But the only "family" I had was my work colleagues and we all had independent lives. It finally dawned on me.... I had a new family. I belonged in Sam and Meg's life. I was the third wheel, but I never felt that way with them. Was I a mother, aunt, or older sister? I wondered which.

There were evenings here and there when I would remain after hours and enjoy dinner with Sam after I fed Meg. That gave him time to leave the worries of work behind and adjust to home. In hindsight I may have done this one time per week. Sam and I would talk about Meg and how content, even happy, she seemed to be. We also talked about ourselves, and I shared my stories with him. There was a warmth in our friendship and my heart and spirit uplifted my self-interest. Maybe I could enjoy a social life again? Maybe I could even have a boyfriend? Those thoughts made me shake my head and laugh. I talked to myself and dropped the subject of a future romance immediately. But the hope in me continued to grow. I had Sam to thank for that.

At an in-service one evening Anna took me aside to ask me about the job. I updated her on my activities and Meg's seeming happiness. I talked about Sam and his work. After a short chat, Anna asked me about my overall dedication to the family. "Are you becoming too involved with the job? With Meg? Or with Sam?" she asked.

The tone and volume of her voice expressed her greatest concern was about the relationship with Sam. I was dumbfounded! I couldn't believe that anyone would even think that! Then the thought exploded in my mind. Did I think that? Oh, my gosh. I spoke to Anna about the weekly dinners with Sam, noting that we were just friends and we talked about Meg and my day with her. I told her he shared his workday and its problems with me. We were friends. She accepted that with a smile and a nod then went about talking to the others who were around. In-services were fun and educational while still conducting business. I did not expect what had just occurred.

After some self-searching, I backed off on the dinners a bit – going once every other week. Sam said nothing to me about it, which I was relieved to find. It bothered me to limit my time with him. I brought that to my own attention and dealt with it.

One evening when I was staying for dinner, Sam and I ended up discussing love. During it, he reminded me of the marriage vows that are generally taken, specifically the "for better and for worse" and "in sickness and in health" promises to each other. He was much more of a person of Christian faith than I was at the time, but in listening to him talk about this, I felt the Spirit in him saying those words. He believed in and intended to keep those promises to Meg. Although I had no firsthand knowledge of it, I assumed that she intended to keep those promises to him. I had a great deal of respect for Sam. As I was leaving the house to walk home after dinner and our "talk," he reached out and took my hand in his. "Thank you for being such a close and wonderful friend. God sent you to this home." he said.

I stayed with Sam and Meg as her caregiver and his house-keeper and cook for well over a year. I was always delighted in Meg's smile and laugh. Her murmurs were generally happy ones. But the grunts had a certain meaning to them. They did not come often, but I knew they meant disappointment or anger.

During this time, I generally learned more about the damage that strokes leave behind in those bodies that did not succumb to their destruction. Meg routinely developed UTIs from the indwelling catheter. The medication worked well, and she always bounced back.

I agreed to share taking care of a stray dog that Sam picked up off of the side of a road and brought home with him. Sam wanted company and Meg learned to quietly put up with him sleeping on the bed between them. He also jumped up during the day and washed Meg's face for her from time to time. Their backyard was fenced in so he could go out and enjoy the fresh air and do his business without me or Sam having to leave the house. Sam named him Clyde.

I used Sam and Meg as guinea pigs on occasion when I tried out a new and complicated recipe. Most of the time they turned out well, though sometimes it was a garbage can disaster.

Once Sam was behind on his payments to the Agency. Lizzie ignored the debt for a brief time. I wished that I could pay it for him.

Seasons came and went. We operated like a little content family making their own way along a tough road, but one with bright spots. There was good to be found in it.

When Meg decided it was time for her to go, she went peacefully. Sam and I were with her as the Hospice nurse had alerted us to come to her bedside.

Sam invited me to have dinner with him in a restaurant instead of his kitchen once or twice afterwards. We enjoyed a glass or two of wine together and made each other laugh. Then one day he stopped by my house to tell me that he and Clyde were moving to the town where he grew up. He had relatives and friends in the area. I helped him pack despite the tears that I had to choke back or run to the bathroom to convincingly hide.

I stayed with the Agency and continued to help out in others' homes. I fondly remember Meg and Sam...and Clyde.

Epilogue

THE STORIES you have read are based on fact – real people, real events, real emotions. I, Lizzie, was so privileged to know these people and to be involved in so many lives.

I left the position after seventeen wonderful years. I had no choice but to resign because of State law. I was not an RN. But as I mentioned in the Prologue, it was the best seventeen years anyone could have ever had in their employment. I loved my job.

I have been in touch with the major characters since my departure and we lovingly remember those who have passed, or those with whom we have lost touch. All the beautiful, selfless people who worked with this organization, caring for others in need, went out of their way to provide for them. You will be pleased to know that Isabelle became an RN.

I have to relate two comments by two of my team.

I met with the Nutrition Director three months after I left the agency. She summed the working experience together as "a special moment in time." Speaking here and there with others, I learned that we all felt the same way. Years of working together doing what we loved and cared about in our community truly felt like just one very precious moment. We were a close-knit group who meant a great deal to each other.

While still on the job, I wandered into Anna's office one evening after working hours. She was alone writing her required client notes of the day. When I walked through the doorway, she turned in her chair, looked up at me and said with tears in her eyes, "There is so much suffering in this world."

I will never forget that. I'll never forget the people.

About the Author

In her professional life, Wendy Weaver engaged in two very different professional careers.

Following the direction of her Master of Education in Counseling degree from Penn State University, she worked as a counselor for the addicted in a VA hospital and, later, for difficult youth and families in a treatment center for adjudicated delinquents. She also acted in leadership positions during those times.

Her administrative skills then took her to positions in Home Care, Long Term Care and in Caregiver Safety.

Wendy was the Executive Director in a Home Care agency for seventeen years – those years emotionally generating the strong desire to write *Salt of the Earth*; this book is the result of an eight-year obsession to do so.

Her later career remained in healthcare. She developed, installed, and maintained a Program of All-Inclusive Care for the Elderly (PACE), worked as the Director of Development for a new healthcare equipment manufacturer and later developed the Association of Safe Patient Handling Professionals (ASPHP) with the help of a tremendous Board of caregiving and safety experts.

Wendy is now retired and accepts business consulting projects. She has one married son, Jeremy, who is also a successful business advisor.

Made in United States
Orlando, FL
18 March 2024

44895765R00146